Classic Eateries
of the OZARKS and
ARKANSAS RIVER VALLEY

Classic Eateries
of the OZARKS and
ARKANSAS RIVER VALLEY

· ·

KAT ROBINSON

Photography by Grav Weldon

AMERICAN PALATE

Published by American Palate
A Division of The History Press
Charleston, SC 29403
www.historypress.net

Front cover, clockwise: Oark General Store in Oark. *Grav Weldon*; M.L. Greer at work. *Greer family*; Paul's Bakery in Van Buren. *Grav Weldon*; historical photograph of Pete's Place in Fort Smith. *Miss Anna's on Towson*; George's Majestic Lounge. *Grav Weldon*.
Back cover: Herman's Ribhouse in Fayetteville. *Grav Weldon*; Brown's Catfish in Russellville. *Grav Weldon*; the Excaliburger at the Ozark Café. *Grav Weldon*.

First published 2013

ISBN 9781540222305

Library of Congress CIP data applied for.

Notice: The information in this book is true and complete to the best of our knowledge. It is offered without guarantee on the part of the author or The History Press. The author and The History Press disclaim all liability in connection with the use of this book.

To Richard Allin, never afraid to share his love of Arkansas food, and B.C. Hall, convinced from day one that "young Kat Bear" would find her voice.

CONTENTS

FOREWORD

Note: When the original single book project turned into four regional books, the original foreword would no longer work. Considering how little time was left, I turned to a crazy idea. Enjoy this crowdsourced foreword.

No matter what happens in life, the good, the bad, the happy, the sad—we involve food with it. From the engagement dinner to the potluck meal after the funeral, food is an everyday part of our lives. Food for celebration, food for comfort. This book will give you a little bit of both.

Melinda LaFevers

In this age of brand names and big chains, it is nice to know where to find those "family diners" that the locals like. This book will show you the way to eat like a local, even when you aren't one.

Malinda Godwin

Kat Robinson has combined her love of Arkansas with a love of food and brought together a travelogue of unique places to enjoy while visiting the Natural State. In *Classic Eateries of the Ozarks and Arkansas River Valley*, Robinson takes us on a journey, not just to get a tasty bite to eat but through a cultural history of Arkansas, by visiting diners and restaurants that have served food to Arkansans for over a generation.

Sheree Corbett Burnett

Kat puts an amazing amount of research effort into every slice of pie, plate of barbecue and deep-fried fair food that she tracks down. When she shares her meals with you, her descriptions make you want to crawl into the page and experience the scent, flavor and sight of each dish. Arkansas is truly blessed to have such a dedicated chronicler traveling its byways to search out the best the state has to offer and making sure the rest of the world knows about it too.

Chef Christy Seelye-King, askchefchristy.com

Kat makes Arkansas food sound like the best cuisine in the world! Her descriptions make you want to go down small dirt roads in the middle of nowhere just to have some fried potatoes!

Angie Bradley Stark

She introduced me to R&R Curry. I always thought it was just another BBQ place until I read her reviews. I would never have tried it, but now I can't get enough.

David Backlin, road-less-taken.blogspot.com

Kat Robinson is THE "go-to" person in Arkansas for eatery recommendations. When I read her reviews, I feel like I am in the café, diner or restaurant with her experiencing the sights, sounds, smells and tastes. I know that if a restaurant gets a good review from Kat that it is somewhere I will want to go with friends and family to enjoy a pleasant meal.

Ardee Eichelmann

I've known Kat Robinson since we were both music- and writing-obsessed ninth graders, way back in 1987. We spent weekends writing short stories and listening to the top forty on the radio. She had a chart of each week's top five hanging on her door and would diligently keep up with it. When the State Fair came, I remember trying some of the food. Kat had something to say about each taste, showing a passion for good food even at fourteen years old.

Shannon Frizzell Scrivner

My family uses her previous book, *Arkansas Pie: A Delicious Slice of the Natural State*, as a guidebook while traveling the state.

Malinda Godwin

I was going to write something clean, but I seem to keep thinking about Duck Gumbo in Stuttgart! Mmmm, gumbo.

Joshua Heffy Heffington

I can think of no person more qualified to talk about Arkansas food and restaurants than Kat.

Terri Dutton

Kat Robinson makes me wish that I were a millionaire with a tapeworm—that is, that I had enough money to eat every day at the restaurants she reviews without having to worry much about all the weight gain that would otherwise result.

Guy Lancaster

I can think of no one more qualified than Kat to guide people in their search for the best food and food-related experiences. She's the first person I check with.

Bobby King

I have Kat's book *Arkansas Pie: A Delicious Slice of the Natural State.* It is so interesting. [I] love reading about the history of the pies and the restaurants/diners they come from. I know this book will be just as informative and interesting. Can't wait to read it.

Erin Parker

Out of all the people I have ever met, Kat Robinson is one of those people.
Butch Renfroe, FrontPorchArkansas.com

I became a fan of Kat Robinson's food writing after reading an article about Arkansas watermelon. It brought me to tears—about watermelon! Kat knows Arkansas, knows food and has a gift for stirring up beautiful memories. I cannot wait for her next book!

Sara Willis

Kat Robinson is the definitive food writer for Arkansas (and quite a bit beyond), period. In fact, up-and-coming writers like myself pretty much just want to be her when we grow up. Her word on edibles—their history, stories and, yes, taste—is authoritative.

The thing about food in the Ozarks is its mystery, always a surprise. Without the flash and ad budgets of more metropolitan areas, its best eats are shrouded in legend. People tell stories of driving through to Branson or elsewhere and finding the perfect piece of pie or the most glorious ham sandwich. I believe this book will give some needed permanence to the legends, enabling even more people to discover them for themselves.

Christie Morgan Ison, FancyPantsFoodie.com

There are writers, and then there are writers. The former take you places you might not have been, paint a pretty picture and leave you right smack where you started. The latter take you on a grand adventure, tickle your fancy, whet your appetite and leave you with a yearning to find out for yourselves. Kat is definitely of the latter persuasion. From the Delta plains to the top of the Ozarks, the culinary journey of Arkansas is a rich tapestry of tastes, smells, sights and sounds that many call "home" (with the occasional surprise thrown in just for good measure) so sit a spell, grab a glass of tea, bring your appetites and a smile and enjoy the journey.

Nickie Whittaker II

PREFACE

What you have in front of you is not a cookbook. Well, it does have recipes, but it's really not a cookbook. However, I bet you've located it in the cookbook section of your local bookstore. I'll accept that.

There are many ways to utilize this book. It's meant to give you an overview of the restaurants of the Ozarks and Arkansas River Valley regions of the state of Arkansas and an idea of the terrain you'll cross on your journey. It's a storybook that shares the tales of some of the people involved with these eateries. And it's a travelogue for those wishing to hit the road and journey through the Natural State.

Like its predecessor, *Arkansas Pie: A Delicious Slice of the Natural State*, it contains listings and recipes related to the different locations mentioned in the book. Unlike that book, it has a set of requirements for each entrant. Specifically, the restaurants within are at least twenty years old and are those that are so well known that, if mentioned in a crowd, someone would say "I've been there!" or "I've always wanted to go" while the others would nod.

Enjoy!

Kat Robinson
September 2013

ACKNOWLEDGEMENTS

S pecial thanks go to David Backlin, Darrell Wayne Brown, James Hales, Debbie Horton Arnold, Van Tyson, the Arkansas Highway and Transportation Department, the Arkansas Historic Preservation Program, the Butler Center for Arkansas Studies, the Central Arkansas Library System, the Encyclopedia of Arkansas History and Culture, Eureka Springs Historical Museum, Fort Smith Museum of History, Historic Arkansas Museum, Rogers Historical Museum, Shiloh Museum of Ozark History, Southern Food and Beverage Museum and Tontitown Historical Museum.

Additional thanks go to the many restaurant owners, managers, waitstaff, cooks and chefs who contributed to this effort.

INTRODUCTION

How to Eat Like an Arkansawyer

Before you start talking about restaurants in Arkansas, you have to look at what people here have been eating. We have a long cultural and culinary identity—it's just not a well-known identity. It would be easy to listen to the loudest voices of food writers out there and decide the state is nothing more than a place where you can find barbecue, catfish and cheese dip, but that's not all there is to it.

You have to get deeper, and to do so, you really have to ask the bigger question: how does an Arkansawyer eat?

The question has been raised by many who have sought the definition of dining in Arkansas. Few have ever answered this with any true measure of authority, and for good reason: you can't just present a singular plate of food and call it "Arkansas." We're a state of regions, of differences in terrain and culture and of different ethnicities, religions and politics. We're a crossroads, but we're more than that. From our Native American roots to our southern culture, our home cooks and restaurant chefs have spent generations combining family recipes and traditions with locally grown produce and provisions to craft a unique flavor.

For two hundred years, the Mississippi embayment (part of the great alluvial plain of North America's largest river system) has provided rich, deep soil for growing rice. The Arkansas Delta produces more of the staple than any other state in the Union and more than most other countries. Those same flooded rice fields provide a fantastic winter wetland for ducks, and the highly sought-after waterfowl grace many an eastern Arkansas table.

The Memphis barbecue style has influence here, and you'll probably get shredded pork from a Boston butt on your sliced white bread when you ask for barbecue. Coleslaw on the sandwich is Arkansas's contribution to one of the finest sandwiches in the South.

Many restaurants serve another Arkansas oddity: the Reuben sandwich. The corned beef topped with swiss cheese, sauerkraut and Russian dressing on marbled rye is found on menus in every region.

Cornmeal is another long-running staple, and in the Delta, you can find it often in tamales, served just about anywhere close to the river. Filled with beef or pork and wrapped tightly in cornhusks, these are steamed and served hot, sometimes with chili.

Italian families immigrating to the Ozarks through the Delta brought pasta and sauce-making abilities with them. Spaghetti is a frequent side item in the region and is usually served with fried chicken. Another variation on pasta and sauce is a popular cold side item: macaroni and tomatoes.

Fresh fruits and vegetables dominate the dinner table, especially during the summer months. Purple hull peas, a type of crowder pea, tend to be boiled up with ham or bacon. Fat Bradley County pink tomatoes are served sliced with a little salt. Sweet potatoes are served baked whole or chopped and boiled, served with butter and brown sugar or honey.

Fried cabbage (sautéed in butter in a pan) often accompanies milk gravy–smothered pork chops, and unsweetened or barely sweet white cornbread is served up with collard greens or poke salat and pot likker. Fresh spring strawberries, summer blackberries, peaches and watermelons require little more than a quick washing and slicing before serving.

Smoked meats have been part of the diet since frontier days; smoked hams, bacon and turkeys are still widely served and marketed.

On Fridays, fried catfish is served in abundance, thanks to the state's Catholic influence of fish on Fridays. Hush puppies usually accompany the dish, along with the ever-present condiment of green tomato relish. Fresh fish, such as trout, crappie and bass, are enjoyed year round.

We like our gravy, and we serve it on biscuits and potatoes and, especially, over rice. There's even a variant, chocolate gravy, with dual roots in the Ozarks and the Delta.

On the condiment front, there's homemade chow-chow, with its bits of corn and tomato; bread-and-butter pickles, made from cucumbers; onion and okra pickles; and a vast variety of jams, such as mayhaw, huckleberry, plum, fig, gooseberry and pear. There's apple butter, a smashing of apples and spices put up (canned) and served out over biscuits. And there are dozens of varieties of Arkansas honey and sorghum molasses.

Indigenous pecans appear in everything from sweet potato casserole to pecan pie. And you'll find every sort of pie, from cream pies and meringues to fruit and chocolate versions and even fried pies, all over the state.

Arkansas even has its own brand of ethnic-infused cuisine called Ark-Mex, developed with Mexican influence, that incorporates fresh local tomatoes with beans, rice and peppers for a particularly Arkansas flavor. Most Ark-Mex restaurants also serve their own version of cheese dip.

We have our native foods: squash, beans, nuts, berries and muscadine grapes. Corn was introduced a thousand years ago by the tribes that migrated to the Arkansas River Valley. Bison and elk roamed here until they were hunted to extinction (elk have been reintroduced in the Buffalo National River Valley). Deer, duck and turkey are still harvested by hunters each year to grace tables. Arkansas was a hub for apple growing in the late nineteenth and early twentieth centuries, and the Arkansas Blackapple variety remains popular.

Soybeans have taken hold here, too. We celebrate a variety of fruits and vegetables both at the table and with festivals for peaches, watermelon, grapes, purple hull peas, Bradley County pink tomatoes, strawberries, mayhaws and apples.

And we enjoy it all with our breads—cornbread from white cornmeal baked unsweetened or cornmeal cakes of yellow cornmeal with sugar; big fluffy hot rolls; cathead biscuits (biscuits made large, about the size and shape of a cat's head); monkey bread; jalapeño cornbread; corn pone; johnny cakes; corn sticks—and we like that bread hot and served with butter and sometimes honey.

Try to narrow it down to a single cuisine, and you're missing something. An Arkansas dinner could be a plate of braised wild duck and root vegetables in the autumnal Delta or chicken-fried deer steaks with gravy over rice and butter beans in Lower Arkansas. It could be fried chicken and spaghetti with plenty of bread and butter in the Ozarks, smoked ham and redeye gravy with smashed 'taters and cob corn or a summer meal of fresh tomatoes, fried cabbage, purple hull peas with ham and onion and fresh peaches for dessert. It's no wonder our restaurants come up with so many different dishes; Arkansas offers a vast paint box of flavors on which to illustrate any menu.

Within these pages, you'll learn about the history of restaurants in the Arkansas Ozarks and River Valley. Many of the dishes from home cooks have been reinterpreted by chefs in these restaurants, through daily plate-lunch specials and famous dishes. Other menu items were born of the diner culture that was sparked and grew thanks to the spread of the automobile and the country-crossing routes that span the state, such as U.S. Highways 62, 64, 65 and 71. And still more were brought in by migrations and displacements from military actions, immigration and exploration. Today, this section of Arkansas is home to a wide palate of tastes. Let's go explore it together.

Chapter 1

FRIED CHICKEN, SPAGHETTI AND THE LEGACY OF TONTITOWN

B orn of similar dishes brought across the South from both African and Scottish ancestors, the traditional fried chicken served as "Sunday's best" is still prevalent today, battered and fried either in a cast-iron skillet or a deep fryer.

Throughout Arkansas, the crisp-crusted comfort food is interpreted by chefs and cooks both renowned and obscure. Concentrations of good fried chicken appear in restaurants in select cities here and there; the best is purely a matter of conjecture.

But first, to understand the presence of fried chicken in Arkansas, you have to understand where our food comes from. Before this land was settled by immigrants, the cuisine of Native Americans was based on what was available, and that varied by region. The indigenous species here included squash and beans; corn was introduced a thousand years back. While a large selection of nuts (pecans, hickory, walnuts) grew throughout the state, protein sources varied and included everything from venison and elk to bear and raccoon and whatever else came on foot. Fish was a strong component.

When the settlers came, the easiest livestock was pork. Pigs could root about anywhere, whether in Delta mud or rocky Ozark plateau, and they consumed whatever was available. Chickens were brought as well, though they were more prized for their eggs than their meat. Yardbird was a special-occasion food (what you ended up bringing to the church social), and fried chicken was considered "Yankee Dinner"—a phrase first used here by William Minor Quesenbury, who called visiting Northerners "chicken-eaters."

For the folks of the Delta, fried chicken caught on quickly. Most settlers from Europe were accustomed to having their chicken roasted or stewed—traditions that date back to Roman times. The Scottish folk, however, are believed to have brought the idea of frying chicken in fat to the United States and eventually into the Arkansas Delta in the eighteenth and nineteenth centuries. Similarly, African slaves brought to the South were sometimes allowed to keep chickens—which didn't take up much space—and they put them to grease spiced with pepper and paprika. And that grease? Immersion in hot oil in a cast-iron vessel is far less time consuming and requires fewer resources than baking. Hence, that propensity for jointing and processing chicken with the skin on, dipping in flour and buttermilk and egg and dropping into a hot skillet of grease or lard took hold.

So that explains the Delta. But why are some of our best-known chicken restaurants located on the opposite end of the state, way up in the Ozarks? Well, that has to do with the Italians and grapes.

See, Lake Village is where a group of Italian immigrants came in back at the end of the nineteenth century, in 1895 and 1897. They wanted to make a good home for themselves here. Problem was, they came for the opportunity to buy into the Sunnyside Plantation—a development idea of New York philanthropist Austin Corbin, who planned to sell ten- and twelve-acre plots to new area colonists with payments stretched out over several years. These new arrivals became tenant farmers, and though they had planned to come to America and grow fresh produce, they discovered that slow transportation in the area and the type of soil they had to deal with was far more suitable to cotton and corn—neither of which these farmers knew much about. Add in the humid climate, mosquitoes and disease, and you have a recipe for failure—125 died in the first year.

There were good things, though. Over the couple of years these immigrants were in Chicot County, they shared their Italian gastronomic identity, teaching pasta and sauce making to the residents, and picked up the knowledge of how to properly prepare poultry for the pan.

The hard life was too much for many of the new immigrants, who quickly turned their thoughts on creating a means to escape the tough conditions. In 1898, some forty families chose to follow Father Pietro Bandini out of the Delta. They traveled to the north and west and braved the Ozarks and the Boston Mountains to settle in the northwest corner of the state. The town they founded, Tontitown, was named after seventeenth-century explorer Henri de Tonti.

The first year they were there was as harsh as their sojourn in Lake Village. The families came in waves starting in January, not the best time of year to start a farm. By March, the community had its first death but also its first birth, and its members were hopeful.

They grew apples, peaches, strawberries, whatever vegetables they could force up through the rocky soil and eventually turned to the grapes that would make the town famous—yes, grapes.

It wasn't easy. Ozark natives didn't take well to the Italian immigrants at first, but the tenacity of these tightknit families was undeniable and, quite frankly, admirable. And that fried chicken and spaghetti combination, irresistible and served up with bread and butter, over time brought the masses to the restaurants that were born from the Tontitown settlement.

THE TONTITOWN GRAPE FESTIVAL

That summer in 1898, after the first crops came in, the whole community celebrated with what locals say was the "best meal that could possibly have been served" being shared by all. More than a century later, that's marked as the very beginning of the Tontitown Grape Festival.

Grapes and apples solidified this community. The harvests from both helped pay the mortgage on the land that Father Bandini had arranged for the original families, and when the apples failed, the grapes sustained. Everyone had a grapevine in his yard, and by the 1920s, there were commercial vineyards throughout the area. Yes, there was wine, but there was also juice, which kept Tontitown from drying up during the Great Depression. Today, most of the grapes go for commercial juice, though there's one new winery that's trying to reclaim the wine heritage.

Each year in August, the entire town shows up for almost a week of festivities on the grounds of St. Joseph's Church. There are vendors selling every sort of art and craft, a carnival, a legendary book sale, fun and games and the "Eye-Talian" Spaghetti Dinner.

Well, it's not spelled like that, but folks around those parts do call it that—mostly the older folks and those who want to be ironic about things, truthfully. Still, it is of legend, a celebration over what is essentially the dinner plate of the Arkansas Ozarks. You buy your tickets in advance for a certain time, and right before that time, you go wait in line outside the church gymnasium. Over the course of several nights, some eight thousand people will participate in the traditional feed.

The spaghetti is made by hand for weeks in advance and dried on wooden racks. The sauce cooking begins several days before. What you get is a deep, rich and spicy sauce served over pliant noodles with a couple of pieces of Italian American–influenced, soul food–worthy fried chicken—that, and a salad, a roll and iced tea.

Tontitown still celebrates that passion, but that doesn't mean you have to wait until August each year to enjoy the combination or the Italian influence. There are still several classic restaurants in Tontitown and nearby Springdale that serve up the specialty, and you can find it all over the Ozarks.

MARY MAESTRI'S

The oldest of the restaurants still serving the area is still with us, though it has moved from Tontitown to Springdale.

In 1904, there was a young Irish woman by the name of Mary Ritter who attended the Tontitown Grape Festival. There, she met Aldo Maestri. They fell in love, and soon, Mary moved in with the Maestri family, where she learned how to make pasta and sauces and all the good dishes Aldo loved.

In 1923, the grape harvest failed, and the young couple turned to selling dinners out of their home instead. Aldo made wine, Mary made the food and word spread about the place way out in the country where you had to have reservations to come eat. Still, at seventy-five cents a person for all the pasta, chicken and bread you could eat, it was deemed well worth it.

The Maestri family didn't have a telephone, but they did have a friend with a plane. He would drop reservations he took by phone over their place, and the restaurant prospered madly. Mary served up so much chicken she had to eventually sign on with a processor in town; before then, she caught and cleaned the birds from the farm herself.

Mary and Aldo opened a larger restaurant in 1947 with their son, Edward, who was quite an innovator. He built machines that would roll and cut the pasta for Mary and figured out how to properly freeze meat sauce and spaghetti, and then he sold it to stores to sell to their customers. Remember, this was before the TV dinner, at a time when the only frozen foods in the grocery stores there were strawberries.

Aldo passed away in 1959, and in 1968, Ed took on the responsibilities of teaching the business to his twenty-two-year-old son, Daniel, with the help

Mary Maestri's in Springdale. *Kat Robinson.*

of his mother. But in 1977, Ed died suddenly. Mary passed three years later. Daniel built a bigger home and restaurant that year, since the old one was structurally unsound.

The 1980s and 1990s were tough times, but the restaurant managed to persevere. In 2010, the Tontitown location was forced to close, but two years later, the eatery opened up in the former Front Porch Diner location in Springdale as Mary Maestri's Italiano Grillroom and Aldo's Wine and Coffee Bar. There, it is thriving.

Today, Daniel's three sons are heavily involved in the business. A lot has been added to the menu, including steaks, sandwiches, seafood and spumoni. Mary Maestri's no longer serves the bone-in chicken beside the spaghetti. Instead, it's chicken parmigiana, with a fried chicken breast served under the sauce over noodles. But it's still that same great sauce that brought travelers to the Maestri's door more than eighty-five years ago.

THE VENESIAN INN

The same year that Mary Maestri's moved to large digs, another Italian operation started up. This one's become a legend of its own, especially to Arkansas Razorback fans. Of course, I'm talking about The Venesian Inn, the little beige building by the road in Tontitown that has changed little since

25

The original flyer for The Venesian Inn still hangs on the wall. *Courtesy The Venesian Inn.*

The Venesian Inn. *Grave Weldon.*

opening day on June 28, 1947. How do I know that date? It's posted on the flyer on the wall inside the little place, complete with these lines:

Where You Will Find Up-to-Date Cabins.
Excellent Meals Consisting of Italian Spaghetti, Ravioli and Fried Chicken.
Private and Semi-Private Dining Rooms
Also Filling Station with Phillips 66 Products

The cabins and filling station are long gone, but today, you can still go in and sit at the wooden tables installed by Germano Gasparotto in 1947, the year the place opened. You can still have your fried chicken and spaghetti, and you're still going to get far more spaghetti than you can reasonably eat in one sitting. The sauce is spicy and packed with beef, the meatballs are baseball sized and the waitresses will still bring out those slightly sweet rolls with real butter for you to enjoy with your repast.

Gasparotto, a native Italian, ran the place a few years before handing it off to more native Italians—John and Mary Granata. They ended up passing it down to their daughter Alice Leatherman, whom customers still remember as being a prankster. In 1992, she in turn gave it over to her nephew, Johnny Mhoon, and his wife, Linda. Today, Linda runs it with her daughter, Monica Gipson.

The Mhoons, like those who preceded them, are dedicated to continuing the made-from-scratch dishes that sparked the location's popularity. Of course, this means a lot of the shortcuts other Italian restaurants take don't exist, and that might make for a longer wait. But people don't seem to mind. They keep coming back, generation after generation.

The Venesian Inn doesn't serve alcohol, but it does allow you to bring in your own bottle of wine, a nice touch for those who want it. And if you're a guy, you should know that the men's room is actually across the parking lot—sorry about that.

MAMA Z'S

The tradition continues in the newer restaurants as well. Mama Z's is the youngest of Tontitown's family Italian restaurants. It opened in 1988 with Edna Zulpo and her daughters—Lisa, Yvonne and Julie—incorporating the recipes of Edna's grandmother Vivian Morsani. Today, Julie Zulpo-

Mama Z's in Tontitown. *Grav Weldon.*

Browning is in charge of the operation, overseeing pastas and sauces made from scratch.

Mama Z's is particularly known for its pasta, which is also sold by the register for folks to take home and cook up at their leisure. It's also known for great fried chicken and for a marvelous, fluffy coconut meringue pie. The place tends to pack out at lunch, and it's not uncommon to see folks duck in and grab their orders to go, which is good, since no reservations are ever taken.

NEAL'S CAFÉ

Neal's Café in Springdale has dropped the spaghetti altogether. Honestly, no one's been able to figure out if it ever served spaghetti in the first place.

Opened in 1944 under the motto the "Best of Better Foods," Neal's has become a landmark. It's hard to miss the pink building west of the big neon sign on U.S. 71 B (Thompson Avenue) in Springdale. It's pink on the inside, too, with green tile on the floor, although the tile used to be pink as well. Neal's Café is apparently secure in its masculinity.

It does seem rather masculine, with the rifles on the walls; the deer, elk and bison heads on the walls; the massive stone fireplace; and the manly chandeliers. Neal's was rockin' the Lodge look before Lodge had a name.

Why the pink? Well, when Toy and Bertha Neal started up the restaurant, she insisted it be painted her favorite color. It balances out the Lodge feel.

Still, forget all of that. What you need to go eat at Neal's is the chicken—it's still fried in an iron skillet, one of the few places in the state that's not battering the bird and throwing it in the deep fryer. This produces an especially crisp, tight-crusted bird with little grease.

Neal's Café in Springdale. *Grav Weldon.*

Little has changed over the years at Neal's Café in Springdale, except the furniture. *Top image from historic postcard; bottom image Kat Robinson.*

Neal's is also the only place in Arkansas I know of that is still serving pulleys—no, not those wheels that make hauling things easier. I'm talking about the *v*-shaped chicken part that covers the wishbone. While most restaurants have gone to serving their breasts whole, Neal's still dismembers those chickens, and that includes cutting the pulley and frying it. And, oh, it's good.

The pies are legendary, especially the ones with meringue. You can get a fried ham sandwich there or, better yet, a side of that marvelous apple-walnut salad while you're there. And Neal's offers all-you-can-eat fried catfish, whenever you want it, as long as the café is open.

AQ CHICKEN HOUSE

Springdale's go-to place for the fried chicken and spaghetti combination is, hands down, the AQ Chicken House. Once again, we're talking pan-fried chicken but on a grand scale.

The original Springfield location began in 1947, back when Thompson Avenue was a little dirt road. Chickens were raised, killed, cleaned and processed right behind the building—talk about fresh. You could get half a bird for sixty-five cents and a cup o' joe for a nickel.

AQ, which stands for Arkansas Quality, was the brainchild of Roy Ritter, who sold "Southern Fried Chicken" to the masses (or really, the dribs and drabs) that found their way up Highway 71. He eventually sold the operation to Frank Hickingbotham (who went on to create TCBY Enterprises Inc.) and Ron Palmer, who owned it for seventeen years before they sold it to Dick Bradley in 1998. If you ever get the chance to meet Dick, you might be surprised. For someone at the three-quarters-of-a-century mark, he's tan and fit and marvelously happy in appearance. He's done chicken his whole life, first working in commercial eggs and then in chicken growing for Tyson before going into the restaurant business. To purchase both AQ locations, he sold his chicken farm in Lincoln. He may not have a college degree, but he's plenty smart.

AQ's had its celebrity run-ins. Frank Broyles dined there often during his nineteen-year run as Head Hog for the Razorbacks. Bill Clinton ate there, of course, and George W. Bush once got takeout for Air Force One.

And why wouldn't they? The menu is full of Arkansas favorites and offers chicken cooked just about every way imaginable. There are the

Historic AQ Chicken House postcard. *Used with permission from the collections of the Shiloh Museum of Ozark History, Springdale, Arkansas.*

AQ Pickle-Os (fried pickles), of course, and then there's barbecue chicken, chicken on salads, chicken and dumplings, chicken quesadillas, Hawaiian chicken, chicken Parmesan, southwest chicken, chicken Alfredo, chicken-fried chicken smothered with gravy, Cajun chicken, Butter Crust chicken breast, chicken livers, fire-roasted chicken and chicken over the coals.

But the one that's endured over all this time is the original AQ pan-fried chicken. And the best way to have it, in my humble opinion, is in the AQ combo. It's three pieces of chicken (light or dark, your choice) and spaghetti, smothered in a mild marinara, Parmesan, mozzarella and provolone.

No matter what you get, it's all served up with cloverleaf rolls and butter, with strawberry preserves and local honey on the table. And it's all very reasonably priced. Oh, there's apparently also catfish, ribs and steak on the menu, but I've never really had a reason to notice those.

MONTE NE INN CHICKEN RESTAURANT

There's one more famed fried chicken place to talk about that's not too far out from Springdale: the Monte Ne Inn Chicken Restaurant. It's the only restaurant in the vicinity of the ruins of Monte Ne and the only steady restaurant on the way out to the Horseshoe Bend Recreational Area run by the Army Corps of Engineers on Beaver Lake (though there is a small

Inside Monte Ne Inn Chicken Restaurant. *Grav Weldon.*

seasonal pizza joint along the way). The menu never hits the table at the eatery because if you go, you're going to get the exact same thing everyone else is going to get: a filling family-style dinner of fried chicken and all the fixings, brought to your table and refilled until you are stuffed. Just don't forget to make reservations.

Open since 1975, the restaurant has survived with a simple business model. Six nights a week (and Sunday afternoon), guests show up at their appointed time. You're given a seat and a bean crock—hot bean soup. A table laden with delicious home cooking follows: bowls of fried chicken, string beans, corn, mashed potatoes, gravy and coleslaw, small containers of apple butter and creamery butter and a fresh soft loaf of bread. It's a feast, and you can have as much as you want.

The community's name, Monte Ne, comes from the resort built there between 1901 and 1930 along Big Spring. The resort was the brainchild of a man named William Hope Harvey. He earned the nickname "Coin" and was one of those guys who had his thumb in every pie. He brought the only presidential convention ever held in Arkansas here and ran for president. He was responsible for Monte Ne, and he founded the Liberty Party and, on a more sedate and important note as far as we're concerned, the Ozark Trails Association under the idea that more people would come to the resort if there were good roads to make it there. Check out Allyn Lord's book **Historic Monte Ne** for an interesting read about an interesting man and a community founded around this resort.

Monte Ne's ruins, by the way, were partially inundated when Beaver Lake was filled in the 1960s. You can still see the ruins today, including a three-story tower and basement of the old Oklahoma Row and a fireplace and some stairs from Missouri Row. Harvey's remains are interred with his son's and copies of his books in a tomb on private land nearby.

The catch is that you put your own food on your own plate. The family-style service means it doesn't matter if you have two or twenty at your table; that's just how the meal is served. I have seen different couples seated together as strangers who walked away as friends when the meal was over. It's marvelous.

After I looked back through all the Ozark greats in fried chicken, I noticed one other thing. Every one of them offers soft rolls and the butter and honey to go along with them. I don't think that's an accident.

Honey and bread are something that's been a tradition here as long as bread has been leavened in these parts. Arkansas is blessed with good bees and good honey and an eye for getting that honey to the table. But that's a story for another time.

Chapter 2

OLD U.S. HIGHWAY 71 AND THE METROPOLITAN OZARKS

U.S. Highway 71 was first designated as a major north–south route through the United States back in 1926. Today, the route runs from south Louisiana all the way to the Canadian border, traversing Arkansas's western border for three hundred miles. For most of its existence, it's remained two lanes, and the part that runs through northwest Arkansas has tied five towns together: Bentonville, Rogers, Lowell, Springdale and Fayetteville. North of this bustling metropolitan area lies the golf-friendly retirement community of Bella Vista and the border with Missouri. South of Fayetteville, the highway winds through the Boston Mountains and communities such as Winslow and Mountainburg before sliding down into Van Buren and Fort Smith.

In the 1990s, a new stretch of interstate was constructed from Alma to just south of Bella Vista. Upon its completion, the metropolitan section of U.S. 71 was rerouted to run concurrently with I-49. The old section from Bentonville through Fayetteville was resigned U.S. 71 B.

South of Fayetteville, U.S. 71 runs to the east of the new interstate. Once the major route from Little Rock to the northwest, the bypassed highway is now ideal for motorcyclists and those who want to see a bit more of the Ozark highlands.

Bentonville is far from the heart of Arkansas. Today, with I-49 to take you up from I-40, it's about a four-hour drive from Little Rock. Before I-49, it was a trip up U.S. 71 and through several downtowns, a five- to six-hour journey.

If you say Bentonville to other folks, they're undoubtedly going to mention Walmart and Sam Walton to you. Yes, ladies and gentlemen, Bentonville is home to the headquarters for the retail giant. But these past few years, it's taken on a new identity with the creation of the Crystal Bridges Museum of American Art and a bustling downtown square that's been dubbed "21st Century Mayberry." The city is expanding and filling in with art galleries, bike paths and dozens of new restaurants. But there are a good number of restaurants that have been around through all the changes and are still going quite strong.

FRED'S HICKORY INN

Many of the restaurants in this book were started by young folks who had a vision. Fred's Hickory Inn started with a couple that was retiring at the end of other careers.

Fred and Lou Gaye retired to Bella Vista in 1969. Fred had been a petroleum engineer, and the couple had moved about quite a bit, spending time in thirteen different countries. When it came time to settle, the couple decided to chase a lifelong dream. Fred and Lou purchased the Wildwood Camp, a couple acres along Walton Boulevard (the local name for U.S. 71B). Now, there wasn't much to the property, just a couple abandoned buildings on top of a hill, but Fred saw value in the place.

As Sherry Mendenhall relates, "Fred told Lou he found this wonderful place to build a restaurant, and Lou thought he had lost his mind, 'cause the weeds had grown up almost taller than the building." But the weeds were cut and the building renovated, and into the kitchen they both went. Fred smoked the meats, Lou created the side dishes and thus was born Fred's Hickory Inn in 1970.

"Fred used to drive up here in the mornings on his lawnmower," Mendenhall says, "with his Chivas and soda in one hand. They had a dog named Chivas that would ride the lawnmower with him. So he would come up and put the meat on, and then, they would come back in the early afternoon. Lou would make her meatballs and her spaghetti sauce, and then, they would open at five o'clock."

Fred's Hickory Inn in Bentonville. *Kat Robinson.*

A lot of history has happened inside the cabin on the ridge. In Sam Walton's book *Made in America,* it's mentioned that the Walmart founder threw a surprise sixtieth-birthday party for his wife there. Walton told Robin Leach on *Lifestyles of the Rich and Famous* that Fred's Hickory Inn was his favorite restaurant. Bud Walton apparently agreed to donate the money for the arena at the University of Arkansas over dinner there.

Sherry Mendenhall is the owner these days. She seated Sam Walton on her very first day on the job. She worked there for twenty-one years before buying the place in 2005. She'll give you a list as long as your arm of famous folks who have come through the door: Jonathan Winters, Garth Brooks, Paula Abdul and Denver Pyle among them. The entryway is wallpapered with signed photographs of all the celebrities.

And yes, there's a Clinton connection. Sherry says before Bill Clinton officially announced he was running for president, he attended a retirement party there and quietly let the attendees know his intentions.

Fred's specialty of smoked sirloin is still the top draw. If you've never had a smoked sirloin, it's different. With hickory flavor all through the meat, it is sort of like a wood smoke–flavored prime rib. I've never encountered that flavor elsewhere. Barbecue meats at Fred's aren't sauced; they're dry rubbed with sauce on the side, if you really want it.

Lou still comes in. She's ninety-eight years old, and she still enjoys greeting the customers. And there are a lot of them. Any weekend evening, it's hard to find a spot to park in the gravel-and-concrete lot behind the building. And forget about getting in when there's a Walmart shareholders meeting going on. The restaurant was founded eight years after Sam Walton got going and a year after the chain was incorporated. The two grew up side by side there in Bentonville.

The Station Café

Station Café may not have a Clinton incident to brag about, but it has had its share of famous folks within, thanks to its history. See, the hole in the wall on the Bentonville square has previously been a shoe store, a drugstore, an ice cream parlor and a theater. Back in the 1950s, the stars of the silver screen could be seen inside Cozy's Theater. There are some folks who think the place is haunted. That hasn't been my experience.

In 1993, the place was reopened as The Station Café. It's sometimes called the Filling Station, which is sort of funny, since I don't believe it's ever been involved with gasoline. The big menu items are the Steakburger and Freedom Fries. The burger's been named one of the best in the state by different publications here and there.

But what sets it apart for me is the walnut pie and the walnut cheesecake. There's nothing quite like them.

Mind you, inside The Station Café, it's tight, with two rows of booths on the sides and one through the center. You walk to the back to order and get your own drink. However, there are also great little patio tables and chairs outside offering a great vantage point for people watching.

Glasgow's Mexican and American Foods

Glasgow's Mexican and American Foods has been a Bentonville standard since 1964. Back then, it was south of town on U.S. 71, just past what was called Rainbow Curve. There wasn't much around in the '60s, but today, Glasgow is surrounded by different businesses, hotels and banks. And from what I've been told, not a dadgum thing has changed inside the old stone

The Station Café in Bentonville. *Kat Robinson.*

Glasgow's Mexican and American Foods in Bentonville. *Kat Robinson.*

building. Not the old black pleather booth seats, not the red lamps and not even the old marlin hanging on the wall.

The marlin was a catch by Glasgow's founder, J.D. Glasgow. He and his wife, Connie, were on a fishing trip in Mexico when he landed it.

The menu's not much different from those days either. It's a representation of the Ark-Mex style of dining with enchiladas, tacos, refried beans and other specialties along with steaks, burgers and the like. It's certainly a trip down memory lane.

SUSIE Q'S MALT SHOP

Susie Q's did not get its name from the Dale Hawkins song of 1957 (nor from the remake by the Rolling Stones in 1964 or the slow groove Creedence Clearwater Revival put on the hit in 1968). The name comes from a potato cutter. At least, that's what Mildred Head is claimed to have said about the little stand alongside Second Street in Rogers.

The Head family built the structure as a fruit market, but when her cousin's business failed, Mildred took over the place. The year was 1960. A friend of hers introduced her to a man from the Meadow Gold Ice Cream Company (which doesn't exist anymore in the area), who helped her choose her equipment, got it ordered and even stuck around to see the business take off. Challenged with naming the new place, Mildred went with the name on the curly fry cutter. Thus, Susie Q's Malt Shop was born.

Mildred ran the place until 1972, when she let her son J.B. take over. She continued to work there until 1999, greeting customers and helping out. She passed away in 2002.

J.B. and his wife, Patti, kept it up, changing very little about the restaurant or its menu. In 2004, they sold the operation to cousin Patsy Head Simmons, a local realtor who'd been hanging out at Susie Q's practically since she was born.

Today, the neon still shines, and the restaurant thrives. And it's become known for the Big Pig, one of the state's few pork tenderloin sandwiches. The ice cream is cold, the shakes are a little frosty and that trip down nostalgia lane has to be taken in the warmer months, since the family shuts the place down during the winter.

Susie Q's Malt Shop in Rogers. *Historic photo by James Hales.*

Interstate 49 has changed the way folks travel through northwest Arkansas. That quick trip will get you from Bella Vista and the Missouri border down to Alma near Fort Smith on I-40 in under two hours, even with the worst traffic, except on Razorback weekends, but that's Hog fans for ya.

U.S. 71's route may have been bypassed, but its business loop through the metropolitan area is still home to many of the classic restaurants of the state.

Fred's Hickory Inn and Glasgow's Mexican and American Foods both rest on U.S. 71B. Susie Q's Malt Shop sits just a couple of blocks north of where the highway turns for Bentonville. Head south, and you'll come to more greats. In Lowell, you pass by Ron's Hamburgers, an outpost of the Tulsa chain that's been open since 1975.

Further down, you head into Springdale, passing first AQ Chicken House and then Neal's Café. If you were to turn right onto Sunset Avenue (U.S. 412

westbound), you'd soon come to football-fan favorite Susan's Restaurant, which serves great breakfast and pie and a chili omelet that can't be beat. If you were to turn off U.S. 71 at Robinson Avenue (U.S. 412 eastbound), you'd find yourself not far from the new location of Mary Maestri's, recently relocated from Tontitown.

Crossing over into Fayetteville, you pass the gigantic commercial complexes that have sprung up over the past decade or so. On the other side of the Fulbright Expressway, there's a Village Inn that claims it makes the best pie in Arkansas (as a chain, it didn't even make the book *Arkansas Pie*), an outlet for Arkansas-based BBQ chain Whole Hog Café, another for the Flying Burrito Company and several little chains here and there.

HERMAN'S RIBHOUSE

And then you come to Herman's Ribhouse, the latest restaurant in a building that rightfully claims to be the oldest continuously operating restaurant in Fayetteville. Tucked tight to the road, the whitewashed building with the screen door and the roof with its multiple A-frames sits in the middle of a gravel parking lot, which is usually packed any Tuesday through Saturday at dinnertime and always all day on a Razorback game weekend.

Before Herman's, the Royal Oaks Tavern was the name of the restaurant. It was run by Rolla H. Finch, who bought an acre and the little white farmhouse from P.M. Pace, who had owned it since 1929. On New Year's Day 1964, Herman Tuck opened the restaurant again, a place outside the city limits to come get meat smoldered over hot hickory coals. The first menu contained nine items: five sandwiches, a large T-bone, barbecue chicken and a plate and a rack of ribs.

Herman Tuck eventually retired, first leasing the restaurant to Bruce and P.J. Barnes and then selling the place to Benny Spears in 2000. Mr. Tuck's still hanging around today, and the recipes he developed are still in use, including the salsa that's served with a bowl of saltine crackers to every customer who comes in today. Bruce Barnes added the steak and its seasoning to the repertoire, along with the shrimp and the baby back ribs.

Herman's was a place to be seen, and over the years, about every wall of the place was covered with photos of various Herman's customers. But on Christmas 2004, the place caught fire. In the wake, new owner Benny Spears

Herman's Ribhouse in Fayetteville. *Grav Weldon.*

brought in new equipment and built an outdoor deck. Benny wanted a lot from the place, and his final wish was that it carry on.

Yes, dear friends, here's where the story gets sad. Benny Spears was shot and killed outside his home by Fayetteville police officers one night in 2005. He had apparently entered his home security system code incorrectly once and then entered it accurately. The security folks called police, and when they showed up, he walked out of the house with a shotgun. Whose fault it was has been discussed at length elsewhere, but the sad fact is, he died.

Shelby Rogers, one of the partners in the operation, stepped forward and ran it for the next several years. In 2013, she sold the restaurant to Nick and Carrie Wright. Nick worked his way up from dishwasher over seventeen years. He and Mr. Tuck both mention that the assistance over the years of Don Tyson kept the place going strong—yes, that Mr. Tyson, the president of Tyson Foods, who passed away back in 2011. He kept the place stocked with fresh beef, chicken and pork and invested both in the business and the people who kept it going.

The comment I hear the most often about the place is how constant Herman's Ribhouse has remained with the passage of time. There are still red- and white-checkered tablecloths on the tables, bowls of hot water with slices of lemon brought to wash your fingers, menu items with optional "gear" (sliced tomato, green pepper, onion and ham) and those huge steaks. Tootsie Rolls are the only dessert, presented at the end of every meal.

Rick's Bakery

It doesn't take a rocket scientist to know a booming college town like Fayetteville needs a bakery. And it didn't take a rocket scientist to start Rick's Bakery back in 1980. It took a NASA engineer.

Rick Boone had a full-ride scholarship with the air force. After jobs in the space industry dried up with the end of the Apollo program, he needed something to do. That something came in the form of a tiny doughnut shop in a strip mall.

Within a few years he and his wife, Sharon, managed to blow up the business with seven locations. But maybe there is a bit of rocket scientist to Rick. He realized he wasn't making any money with all these little operations here and there, so he scaled everything back to just the one store in that same strip mall.

Well, it's not a tiny little hole in the wall any more. Through a move to another spot in the shopping center and through one expansion after another, Rick's Bakery is now 12,500 square feet of cake-wielding power, a giant in the baked goods industry in Hog Town. There's often a line out the door, and there are more baked goods than you can mention in a minute, even if you're the Micro Machines guy.

Every day, several hundred customers come through the door. Several thousand doughnuts are sold. About half the bakery's business comes from decorated cakes, and just about any time you walk in, you'll see someone tackling a new creation.

Rick's Bakery in Fayetteville. *Grav Weldon.*

To me, what stands out most at Rick's are the colors: bold, bright and sometimes even brash. Every case beams with color, from the sprinkled doughnuts to the eye-popping cakes to almost tie-dyed iced sugar cookies. Rick's Bakery really has become a bright spot—and a necessary stop—along U.S. 71's business route in Fayetteville.

RICK'S IRON SKILLET

Down past Dickson Street, there's another Rick's that packs out on a regular basis, Rick's Iron Skillet. Opened in 1990, it's currently run by the Xiong family. They came on board in 2006 and didn't change a thing. You still get one of the best old-fashioned breakfasts you'll ever find, either on a menu or a buffet.

The menu bears tons of favorites—chicken-fried steak, the magnificent burger, the French toast and the Razorback waffle. Really, whatever you get, it's great diner food.

Its proximity to the University of Arkansas campus makes it a must-stop for Hog fans. A litany of football and basketball coaches have been spotted in the place, including current (as of this writing) football coach Bret Bielema.

PENGUIN ED'S

And then there's Penguin Ed's. It began in July 1993 at the corner of Mission and Crossroads in a little trailer, the brainchild of Ed and Diane Knight. The couple had decided to leave the corporate world behind to take up barbecue, and so they did, with that tiny little trailer that was sometimes ten to twenty degrees hotter inside than it was outside.

In 1996, the business moved into the new shopping center built at the same intersection where the trailer was located (the crossroads of Highways 45 and 265). There are two other locations: the one on Weddington near Double Springs (opened in 2007) and the old B&B BBQ location on U.S. 71B, which opened in 2002. That last location, between Rick's Iron Skillet and downtown, is way off down the side of the road. Just follow that smoke.

One of the
penguin
statues outside
Penguin Ed's
in Fayetteville.
Grav Weldon.

The name comes from the penguins that are just about everywhere. Back when the restaurant was still in a trailer, Ed would put these four papier-mâché penguins on the roof. Sometimes, they'd end up on the picnic tables nearby. People started to give Ed other penguins—stuffed ones, ceramic ones, slightly lewd ones, unusual ones. So when it came time to move into the restaurant space, it was only natural that it be called Penguin Ed's.

The meat is sliced thin; the sauce is paprika spiked and sweet; the hot barbecue sauce sings of mustard and vinegar; and there are Whoopie pies, these big fat cookies glued together with sweet, cloying cream.

GEORGE'S MAJESTIC LOUNGE

Now, there are places off U.S. 71's business route that deserve some respect. One of them isn't a restaurant, but it is the hub of activity around which many restaurants have sparked.

That place is George's Majestic Lounge. Opened in 1927 by George Pappas as a restaurant and bar, it also served as a general store for those in

George's Majestic Lounge in Fayetteville. *Grav Weldon.*

the Dickson Street area. He sold it to Mary and Joe Hinton in 1947, and they ran it until Bill and Betty Harrison purchased it in 1987. Since 2004 it's been owned by Brian Crowne and Suzie Stephens.

George's has a lot of "firsts" and "longests" to put on the wall. It's the oldest continuously operating club and live music venue in the state, it was the first local bar to integrate in the 1950s, it was the first place in northwest Arkansas to offer pizza delivery and the first to offer color television. Acts from Leon Russell and the Little River Band to Robert Cray and even the Tower of Power have performed inside the old store.

George's Majestic Lounge isn't a restaurant, but there's a restaurant inside the business. Yazzetti's serves up Italian dishes, pizza, salads and suds three days a week.

Hugo's

And then there's Hugo's. If you've seen *Cheers*, you know what I mean when I say Hugo's is Cheers in a mountaintop town in the Ozarks. Try not to fall down the stairwell when you come in off Block Street. The place is dark, crowded, cluttered, loud and wonderful.

Opened in 1977 in a basement, Hugo's has become enigmatically synonymous with being a native. The restaurant doesn't advertise, and the only real way you'll find the place without a guide is by peering through your car window for the small neon sign with the down-pointing arrow. You're going to have to circle the block for a parking spot anyway, so just keep moving along.

One of the original owners, Liz Page, is responsible for the dashed-together décor, bringing in all sorts of finds from thrift shops and antique stores. She didn't find the "Typewriters" sign, though; well, I don't believe she did. It seems before it was a restaurant, this space was home to a typewriter shop.

The menu has changed little since opening day. Hugo's was one of the first northwest Arkansas restaurants to offer nachos, and today, there are three varieties on the menu. Burgers have recently come into vogue, and Hugo's gets noticed for all its varieties. By far, it's the Blue Moon burger with its crown of blue cheese crumbles that gets the biggest response. Wine, a full bar and thirty-two beers (six on tap) make it the sort of place that alumni look back on in their later years while they smile to themselves, thinking of college-age debauchery.

You'll find Hugo's down this stairwell, half a block from the downtown square. *Kat Robinson.*

Barnett's Dairyette

You can't get much further west in Arkansas than Siloam Springs. Sharing a border with West Siloam Springs, Oklahoma, this burg hugging U.S. 412 stands as its own town, not just another bedroom community from the I-49/U.S. 71 metropolitan area.

It's worth the ride over from Springdale through Tontitown just to have a burger and a shake at Barnett's Dairyette. First opened in 1957 as a walk-up dairy bar, the place has expanded to include a dining room. Eight burgers grace the menu, along with other favorites, such as foot-long subs and tots. But what you really need to experience are the milkshakes: butterscotch, pineapple, peanut butter, pumpkin in the fall, strawberry pie in the summer and even a green mint chocolate chip version for St. Patrick's Day.

Sky Vue Lodge. *Historic postcard.*

Heading south of town, U.S. 71 is a scenic highway that parallels I-49 all the way down to Alma. The two routes are a world of difference. Over the decade and a half that the newer road has been open, little has grown up near it, making it great for those wanting a quick run or some really fantastic high-up views, but not so much for those looking for a bite.

The Boston Mountain Loop (today's U.S. 71) is a much more intimate, slower road. It may be hard to imagine today, but the two lane curvy road through some of the roughest angles in the Ozark Plateau used to be the primary thoroughfare. On Razorback football weekends, it and the Pig Trail (Arkansas Highway 23, which runs roughly twenty to thirty miles to the east) would be a parking lot.

Before I-49, U.S. 71 was jampacked with opportunities to stay, play and eat. Tourist attractions dotted the roadsides, and there was a good place to pull in and dine around almost every corner. There were great motor court motels, cabins and art stands. It was a fantastic trip.

Since 1999, the communities that once saw thousands of cars pass through each day now see just a few hundred. Most of the restaurants have dried up and blown away, and a few have met an even worse end.

The town of Winslow was one of those hit hardest. It's at about the halfway point between the edge of Fayetteville and the Alma city limits, on the top of a scenic ridge. This used to be a great way stop for travelers, even back as far as the Route 71 designation (often referenced as Trail 71 on postcards). There was a lot at Winslow, including an observation tower at Mount Gayler where you could see for miles, even out as far away as Mount Magazine on the other side of the Arkansas River. There was the venerable Burns Gables, a huge stone lodge offering a bed and food to travelers. There was the Sky Vue Cabins and Café that hung out off the side of U.S. 71 overlooking the valley below. The cabins today have been converted into a bed-and-breakfast.

GRANDMA'S HOUSE CAFÉ

In 1991, Ernestine Shepherd opened the Blue Bird House Café on one of those scenic overlooks. The rich blue painted building drew drivers off the road for good country-style vittles. For ten years, it was a staple, but bad health forced Mrs. Ernestine to close the place down. The traffic drawn away by I-49 didn't help matters.

Eventually, she decided to put the Blue Bird House Café up for sale, and she had a buyer right off the bat—Elaine Bowlin, her own daughter. Elaine and her husband, Jerry, decided to take on the job. They renamed it Grandma's House Café, under the idea that Elaine wanted the place to feel like eating at your grandparents' home. Today, the café is bigger (with a couple of expansions), painted gray and home not only to the good food but also a small crop of rocking chairs out front.

The Bowlins serve up the foods of the Ozarks four days a week on a classic country-style buffet. Breakfasts are of baked ham, fried bacon, sausage, eggs, fried potatoes, biscuits, white and chocolate gravy and pancakes cooked to order. Lunches almost always include baked ham, and you'll find ham, pan-fried chicken, chicken-fried steak, meatloaf, pork chops, barbecue chicken breast, meatloaf and some of the best chicken and dumplings you've ever had in your life. You'll always find mashed potatoes, cream gravy, green beans, corn and brown beans, and the yeast rolls are magnificent.

It's also a fantastic place to find pie. At any time, there are half a dozen pies out on the dessert table—cream pies and fruit pies and meringue, too. The pineapple cream is absolutely to die for. Plus, there's cobbler, which can be anything from apple and peach to strawberry and—well, anything you want can be made into a cobbler.

OZARK MOUNTAIN SMOKEHOUSE

A bit further south, traffic would always snarl in front of an old two-story gray building. The scent of smoking meats would cause even the most satiated of drivers to hit the brakes. This was one of the busiest locations of the Ozark Mountain Smokehouse, a small-run chain with locations all over the Ozarks (I'll tell you about one of the remaining stores in the Russellville chapter). It was open for thirty-six years before closing in 2005, the loss of business to I-49 being cited as a significant decision-maker for the Sharp family, who owned it. The building was purchased and renovated to be a guest lodge, but it suffered major internal damage during a fire in July 2012.

There at Mountainburg, you can still find Artist's Point, the two-story structure on the east side of U.S. 71, overlooking Lake Fort Smith and White Rock Mountain. The gift shop, which has been open since 1954, had to adapt, and to do so, the folks who run the place opened up overnight lodging in the second level.

DAIRY DREAM

Some things don't change. Around the time Artist Point opened, there were the beginnings of the Dairy Dream. The tiny little roadside diner in downtown Mountainburg now sits below the newly constructed dam holding back Lake Fort Smith (doubled in size with an expansion in the early 2000s that also saw the same body of water consume Lake Shepherd Springs upstream; Lake Fort Smith State Park relocated to a higher elevation to accommodate the change). It's a tiny place run by the Wilmoth family, the same family who opened the order window back in 1954. Robert Wilmoth opened the place, and years later, he passed it on to son Jerry, who still runs it with his family. For Mountainburg, the indicator on whether spring has arrived isn't assigned to a groundhog; spring begins the day the Dairy Dream opens up for the season. It closes down each year when the weather gets too nippy for ice cream outdoors.

Dairy Dream in Mountainburg. *Grav Weldon.*

The dish of choice is the Mountainburger, which is a nicely spiced burger with relish, chopped onions and mustard. But the Dairy Dream is probably better known for its old-fashioned ice cream delights, not just sundaes and shakes and freezes, but Purple Cows, Wildcats, Baby Elephants, Silver Saddles, Red Rovers and more.

The crowd that comes through on the weekend shows why the Boston Mountain Loop isn't done yet. Sure, business fell off sharply after I-49 opened. But as *Arkansas Business* shared in a March 6, 2006 article, the Arkansas Highway and Transportation Department noticed an uptick in road traffic, a whole 39 percent from 2003 to 2004. As more traffic came up I-49, more people shared stories about the stunning beauty of the Boston Mountains, and more tourists hit the roads, among them motorcycle enthusiasts and "weekend warriors" looking for another good ride. Without the traffic that peaked in the 1990s, making the highway a winding parking lot, the curves are free to enjoy, and all those bikes that come through have riders who require sustenance. Add in the two local state parks (Lake Fort Smith State Park on U.S. 71 and Devil's Den State Park on the other side of I-49), and you have once again a corridor of delights for travelers who want it all: an enjoyable journey, beautiful sights to take in, adventuresome roads with amenities nearby, places to stay and, of course, places to dine.

JENNY LIND CAFÉ

Highway 71 joins I-40 at Alma and then follows I-540 south through Fort Smith to Exit 12 before diving down toward Greenwood. Its business route splits at I-40, joining U.S. 64 in Alma and through Van Buren before becoming Midland Avenue (with U.S. 64) to downtown. On the other side, it's Towson Avenue until the big curve, then Zero Street before turning south again to join its parent route.

Just south of Fort Smith, off the road a bit, you'll find the little community of Jenny Lind. You can get there via Gate Nine Road, which used to go to the ninth gate of Fort Chaffee, on the installation's southern side. Within that town, you'll find an aging building with an old tin roof. It's stood here for ages, serving as a schoolhouse (a two-story one at that), a grocery store, a dance hall, a shoe shop, a series of restaurants and, finally today, the Jenny Lind Café.

If you've read my other book, you may know this as Bob and Wanda's Jenny Lind Country Café. They had taken over the place in the year or so since I had done my first review there, when it was just the Jenny Lind Country Café. Well, the original folks have purchased it back, and here it is again. There are always good things to eat here.

But let's go back a bit further, to this community. Originally named Actus, the town was dubbed Jenny Lind back in the mid-1800s after the famed opera singer who toured with P.T. Barnum. The schoolhouse at Jenny Lind was constructed late in the nineteenth century. The two-story structure housed all ages.

In the 1930s, after the school had been moved to another facility, the schoolhouse was purchased by a man named Joe Erker. He took off the top story, put a new roof on and opened a grocery store.

I mentioned Gate Nine. There wasn't a Gate Nine until Camp Chaffee was opened in 1941, but once there was, there were soldiers looking for a place to hang out when they had a little leave. Joe's grocery store had a jukebox, and soon, Joe had a dance hall, where these guys could kick back and let things lay loose.

Sebastian County (with the exception of Fort Smith) went dry in 1944, and Joe's dance hall was converted to a shoe repair business. Some years

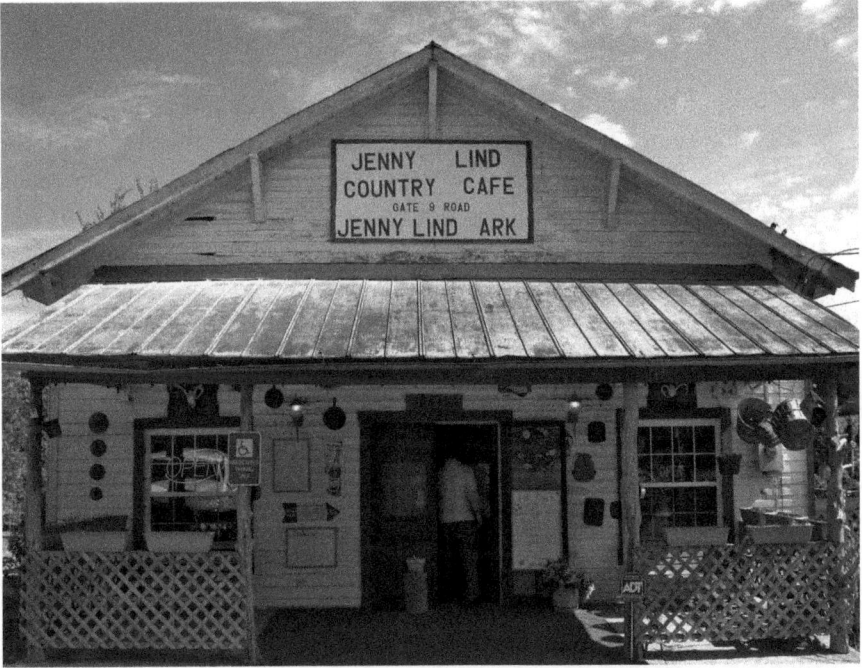

Jenny Lind Café at Gate Nine. *Grav Weldon.*

later he left town, but there are those who believe his ghost lives on at the Jenny Lind Café.

Today, the place is a hodgepodge of this and that, from an old piano to shoes hanging from the ceiling. You'll see bits from the story I just shared with you all over the place. Poems, newspaper articles and the like are nestled in between cola signs, musical instruments, bikes, photographs, posters and piñatas. And above the piano, there's a photo of Joe.

And from time to time, someone cuts off the oven or the air conditioner, spills the sugar or knocks over the bread. Maybe Joe's trying to say something. Or maybe it's all those schoolchildren still looking for that second-story classroom. The Jenny Lind Café has become known for its pie and ample breakfasts and lunches served with a smile. The service may come with a side dish of supernatural, but it's all good.

ROCK CAFÉ

As you head further south and to the far edge of the Arkansas River Valley, U.S. 71 splits again. Its main route mostly bypasses the town of Waldron. Downtown in Waldron, on U.S. 71 B, you'll find a clean red and white diner that's been around since 1936. The Rock Café opened that year and, though it's changed hands numerous times, it's stayed ever since.

Every day at 5:00 a.m., the lights are on and the doors are unlocked for a traditional diner breakfast. Every day at 2:00 p.m. after the lunch buffet, the restaurant is closed, except on Fridays, when it stays open until six o'clock. Every day, you go in and sit below ancient yellowed photographs of stars, from Elvis Presley to John Wayne, and order a meal that's served under wood-paneled walls that have changed little with time.

Each day, the buffet is different. The fried chicken is excellent, and the chicken and dumplings are some of the best you will ever find. Thursday is Mexican fare; Friday is catfish. Little changes from year to year. There's something wonderful to be said about that. Don't get there at 1:55 p.m. and demand lunch, but do get a homemade dessert when you go—and if strawberry cobbler's the offering, you are truly blessed.

Rock Café in Waldron. *Grav Weldon.*

South of Fort Smith, U.S. Highway 71 varies between two-lane blacktop and four-lane freeway, all the way down to the Texas border south of Ashdown. It meanders over the rolling hills at the edge of the River Valley and then through gaps in the Ouachitas before flattening out. It's the most direct route between Texarkana and Fort Smith—at least for the time being.

Over the course of the next several years, development will progress up the border from Texarkana, where right now Arkansas 549 carries a good portion of U.S. 71 up from the Louisiana border. The freeway ends between Texarkana and Ashdown. Recently, the section of interstate north of Alma has been resigned from its old I-540 designation to I-49, and sections are already under construction through Fort Smith and Greenwood to extend this roadway. Eventually, Arkansas 549 will meet I-49 in the middle, and the interstate will stretch from south Louisiana to the Canadian border.

Chapter 3

ARKANSAS CANDY

How Sweet It Is

Candy, sweets, chocolate—they're all popular in the Ozarks. Heck, I figure they'd be popular anywhere. But in a rural area that saw a boom in travelers in the post–World War II era, these desserts became fantastically popular.

It's really no wonder. When you go somewhere on a trip, do you do as they do in Rome and enjoy the local experiences and cuisine? Chances are if you've picked up this book, you certainly do. For the travelers that crossed the Ozarks on Highways 62, 65 and 71, bounced up Scenic Highway 7, forded the Arkansas River Valley on U.S. 64 or Arkansas Highway 22, there was always some place to stop and check out. And for those folks who had family and friends back home, there were souvenirs and thank-you gifts to pick up.

Fudge, hard candies, toffee and brittle travel well. Shops popped up to serve those sweet teeth. Many of them, such as Andy's Ozark Candies in Eureka Springs and Richmond's Mountain Dew Sassafras store in Cotter, are long gone. The tradition remains, and there are still purveyors of these heritage candies today.

The deepest roots of Arkansas chocolate span back to one man: Martin L. Greer (front cover, top left). He started making candy on his family farm all the way back in 1924, selling the sweets in town along with the family's produce. The next year, he was hired on at a Greek candy shop out of Texarkana.

Greer started out apprenticing here and there and worked his way across Texas doing so. He started off with hard stick candy and worked into the softer candies and eventually, in the early 1950s, into chocolate. He moved his family back to Arkansas and started up the Stateline Confectionary in Fort Smith.

Greer inspired not one chocolatier and candy maker, but two.

MARTIN GREER'S CANDIES

One of these was Dr. Martin Greer Jr., his son. Dr. Greer specializes in all sorts of chocolates, brittles and the like in a little shop outside Gateway. If you draw yourself a line between Pea Ridge Battlefield and Eureka Springs, you'll find yourself there, in the middle of nowhere. It's a little, neat white shop that emits the smell of chocolate, a scent that can be picked up a half mile away.

I'm a frequent visitor to Martin Greer's. His wife, Jeanette, dips candies. His elder son, Uriah, has recently become the chief candy maker, and his younger son, Joshua, is learning the craft. And there's something about the chocolate there that keeps me coming back. You know you done good in my world if I gift you with chocolates from Martin Greer's; it is my favorite chocolate, period.

Dr. Greer's thing is making chocolates the same way they were made all the way back in the nineteenth century. He uses recipes from a chocolate cookbook from 1897 called *Rigby's Reliable Teacher*, and the ingredients list includes no preservatives, just cocoa, sweet-cream butter, real vanilla, dry-roasted nuts, fruit preserves and real sugar. He learned well from his father, and by the time he was twenty, he was making

Dr. Martin Greer. *Grav Weldon.*

more than five hundred pounds of chocolate a day. The candy he sold at Silver Dollar City (across the Missouri border to the west of Branson) and Dogpatch USA near Jasper in the early 1960s put him through school at College of the Ozarks down in Clarksville.

Martin Greer isn't just a chocolatier. He's also an animator. For years, he taught art and history at Van Buren High School. The school didn't give a lot of budget for art projects, so he came up with creative ways the students could earn money. They included everything from creating parade floats and puppets to making animated features.

On one of my many passes through the area, my photographer Grav Weldon and I struck up a conversation with Dr. Greer, who asked us what we were interested in. Grav mentioned that he's an animator (Grav's master's degree is in electronic visualization and visual effects, specifically 3-D animation, which makes the fact that he's my photographer a bit of odd trivia), and suddenly, we were welcomed into the back, through the kitchen and a passageway, into a massive studio where Dr. Greer still practices art. He shared with us there his mottled history and about the different animated shorts they created, including a very early animated piece to Ray Stevens's "The Streak," composed of more than four hundred hand-drawn and hand-colored cells.

How did Martin Greer Jr. go from being a high school art instructor to a chocolatier with a doctorate? First, he went back to school, earning a master's in education at Northeastern State in Talequa, Oklahoma, in 1974 and then a doctorate in education at the University of Arkansas in 1979. He became a school superintendent and principal and wrote a couple of art books and a series of short stories. He traveled a great deal and met Jeanette in the Philippines. They moved a bit here and there and ended up all the way over in Knoxville, Tennessee.

In 2000, they came back, and Dr. Greer built the little white chocolate shop on U.S. 62 in the Gateway community. Today, there are three shops: the original, a second operated by family in the Philippines and a third that just opened at Gaskin's Village in Eureka Springs.

KOPPER KETTLE CANDIES

Back in 1956, Kopper Kettle Candies was opened in eastern Van Buren along the Alma Highway (U.S. 64) by the original M.L. Greer and his wife, Betty Greer. Today, it's run by his son Tommy and Tommy's family. The

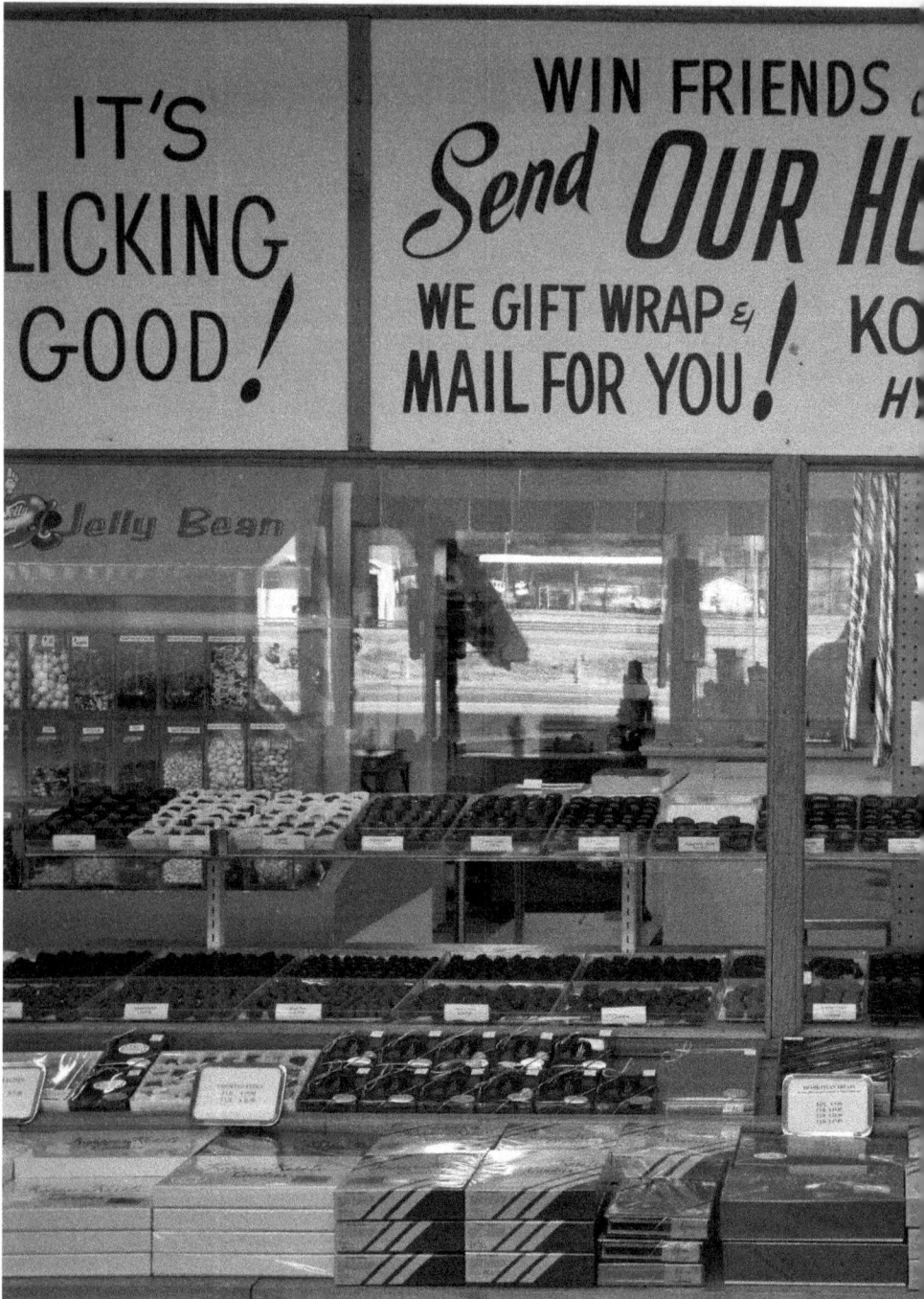

The chocolate racks within Kopper Kettle Candies in Van Buren. *Grav Weldon*.

business was named for a giant, five-foot-wide copper cheese kettle Betty found and purchased more than fifty years ago. The generational store offers more than one hundred different types of confections made there behind a wall of windows, as well as two hundred other sweet items from other manufacturers. The Greers' children and grandchildren are often found working there or in the second location in Fort Smith.

Kopper Kettle Candies range through the candy scale—chocolate-covered cherries, divinity, pralines, toffees, truffles, peanut brittle, fudge, creams, chocolate-covered nuts and something called "Ozarkies," a light vanilla cream center covered by milk and dark vanilla chocolate and pecans. They carry other sorts of goodies made elsewhere, like lollipops and jellybeans.

TWO DUMB DAMES FUDGE FACTORY

Fabulous fudge recipes have been handed down through five generations of family in Eureka Springs, the home of Two Dumb Dames Fudge Factory. Opened by Hallie McGowan Chambers and her daughter, Jonell Powers Sullivan, in 1980, it's become a sweet-tooth destination all its own.

Jonell's daughter Lana and granddaughters BJ and Amanda still run the place today, and great-granddaughters Hallie and AnaBella are learning the crafts of fudge and candy making themselves.

The fudge is of legend rich, unabashedly creamy and in more flavors than dreamed possible. Sucralose versions are ready for the diet- and sugar-conscious to try. But the place is full of far more than fudge. This is an old-fashioned candy store, with everything from jawbreakers to jujubes to turtles and toffee and nostalgia items as well.

The store derives its name from something Hallie's husband said when she and Jonell announced they wanted to start a fudge shop. He declared, "That's the dumbest idea I ever heard of." Never has eating one's words tasted so sweet.

LAMBRECHT GOURMET

Then there are the Smiths of Heber Springs. David and Nancy have been making toffee in some capacity or another for years. David used to be the manager at the famed Red Apple Inn resort (page 214). At the urging of the owners, he started making up the toffee for guests and special occasions. Eventually, the Smiths started selling the toffee at gift shops, and then they started their own company, Lambrecht Gourmet.

It's not just any toffee. It's chocolate coated, and it's becoming pretty well known. In 2012, it won the Gold Medal Award for Top Toffee in America at the Salon International Chocolate Competition, as well as the gold for being a Toffee Partner at the International Taste Awards.

Chapter 4

FORT SMITH AND DINING AROUND THE STATE'S SECOND-LARGEST CITY

Fort Smith could be the state's greatest culinary secret. I hear laughter from residents, but I am not kidding. I'll cite my reasons.

For one, the city benefits from being on U.S. Highway 64, one of the few that cross from one side of the state to the other in a somewhat straight line. Just like its cousin Route 66, Route 64 brought drivers through on their way from the East Coast to the West, starting at Nags Head, North Carolina, and ending on the other side of the Arizona border. Later in this book, we'll discuss one of the most famous travelers along U.S. 64 and the place that made the historic register partly because of him.

Route 64 and Route 71, which traverses the nation from south Louisiana to the Canadian border, used to cross in downtown Fort Smith and run concurrent over the Arkansas River into Van Buren; with the construction of I-540, U.S. 71 was realigned so only its business route follows this path. Today, the two cross in Van Buren. Along both of the original routes and Rogers Avenue (Arkansas Highway 22), you'll find the remnants of the region's diner culture.

The city is also the location for Fort Chaffee, which has influenced the town's culinary culture twice over. Originally built as Camp Chaffee in 1941, the fifteen-thousand-acre facility was created as part of U.S. military expansion before the nation's involvement in World War II. The first soldiers arrived on the property on December 7, 1941—the day the Japanese military attacked Pearl Harbor. It was completed in just sixteen months. In addition to the servicemen who passed through, the camp was also home to three thousand German POWs. Many of the soldiers who came back from the war settled in the area. The camp was eventually expanded to more than seventy-six thousand acres.

In 1956, the camp was redesignated Fort Chaffee. Its most famous short-time resident, without doubt, was Elvis Presley. In fact, many fans know it best as the place where the King received his famous haircut. Today, you can visit the Fort Chaffee Barbershop Museum where the famed event occurred.

Fort Chaffee is also known for having hosted two different groups of foreign refugees. In 1975 and 1976, this is where Cambodian and Vietnamese refugees were processed when they were brought into the United States, with over fifty thousand passing through the base. And in 1980 and 1981, twenty-five thousand Cuban refugees came through.

Thanks to that, the city has the greatest concentration of ethnic restaurants I've found within the borders of the state. There's a high concentration of pho restaurants and various Asian stands and eateries. Most of them have cropped up in the past twenty years or so, with the first generation born in America making its mark. I suspect a few of them will become classics in due time.

There are also a large number of Mexican restaurants, both of the Ark-Mex variety and true Mexican. Immigrants have been passing through for years, heading up the U.S. 71 corridor. Many work manufacturing jobs in town.

There was one more round of refugees that came through Fort Chaffee. Though command of the base was transferred from the U.S. Army to the Arkansas National Guard in 1997 and though around seven thousand acres were turned back to the city for redevelopment around that time, the fort was still in operation. In late August 2005, it became a temporary home to more than ten thousand refugees from south Louisiana and Mississippi in the wake of Hurricane Katrina. Many of those brought to Fort Chaffee ended up making Fort Smith their permanent homes.

The result of all this influx is a wide palate of restaurants, eateries and establishments that cater to the varied tastes of its population. The next century should be interesting there as the city switches from an industrial to a commercial base, with an emphasis on new tourism efforts.

In researching this city, I had a very valuable resource close at hand. This book's photographer, Grav Weldon, grew up in the town and returned there in 2010. Much of the information, and humorous stories therein, comes from research and interviews we conducted while I was working as a full-time food and travel journalist.

ED WALKER'S DRIVE IN

What was life like before the drive-thru restaurant? For those of you younger than I am, that's a question you deserve to have answered. When I was a young child, I can remember the buzz when the McDonald's on University in Little Rock got its first drive-thru window. It was a very big deal.

Just as children my daughter's age find themselves confounded by the thought of a telephone with a cord—let alone one with a rotary dial—they'll probably also wonder what travel was like before drive-thrus. They'll certainly not know what life was like before the drive-in.

Drive-ins differ from drive-thrus in their methodology. A drive-thru has a window where you receive your order while you're sitting in your car. A drive-in is where you order either from a waitperson at a window or from a telecom-driven device and then receive your meal from a waitperson who comes to your car. Sonic is a drive-in chain. Dog 'n' Suds was also a chain of that sort (the last Arkansas location is located in Paragould), as was Breaker Drive-In (two locations still exist here, in Corning and in Monticello).

In Fort Smith, Ed Walker's was the first drive-in, as far as anyone can tell. It was and still is located in a red and white building along Towson Avenue

Ed Walker's Drive In in Fort Smith. *Kat Robinson.*

Ed Walker's is owned by Ted Cserna, who also owns Ed Walker's Too (formerly the Phoenix Drive-In), the Ribeye Steak and Seafood House and MISS ANNA'S ON TOWSON. The latter has its own particular history. Miss Anna's used to be Goodson's on Towson, and Goodson's was another family operation. The original restaurant was on Old Greenwood and known as Goodson's on Cornerstone. The Goodson family has run one restaurant or another since at least the 1970s; in 2011, when both locations were sold, son Mark Goodson started up frozen yogurt hotspot Goody's. Miss Anna's, by the way, is named after Ted Cserna's mom.

It's also well known for its marvelous pies and cakes, a tradition kept over and perhaps even improved from its Goodson's days. In fact, the baking prowess of said store has spread to the other properties in the form of pies and the specialty buns for the five pound burgers at Ed Walker's.

THE RIBEYE (or Rib-Eye, as its sign says—its website and menu have the name as one word) has been around since 1968. Inside the classic exterior, little has changed. Diners still have the choice of a small salad or a hearty cup of vegetable beef soup before the entrée, and the steaks are still fork tender. The restaurant is probably best known for the steaks, but some also laud its fried pickles and a massive chunk of a dessert: the amaretto bread pudding.

The Rib-Eye Steakhouse in Fort Smith. *Grav Weldon.*

in Fort Smith, also known as U.S. Highway 71. Ed Walker's has an awning that spans from the building almost out to N Street, with parking spaces for several vehicles. You pull up and flash your lights, and someone will come out and take your order. They bring it out to you when it's done.

Mind you, the only reason that the awning spans out from the side like that is because the place was a gas station before it was a restaurant.

Ed Walker's has a lot of unique details to it. Opened in 1943, it's currently the longest continuously operating restaurant in the city. It's also the only place in the entire state of Arkansas that offers drive-up beer service. What? Yep, you can drive up and park under the awning, flash your lights, order a beer and even drink it in your car. Wait, how? Well, though Arkansas has no law allowing open containers and no way to fudge it (like Louisiana, where you can visit a drive-thru daiquiri shop, order a daiquiri and get it with a piece of tape over the straw), Ed Walker's has been grandfathered in. Fort Smith is a border city, and this place is seventy years old as of this writing, and as long as the liquor license never lapses, this one exception exists.

But that's not why most folks come by. The big draw is the french-dipped sandwich, which is legendarily good. It's tender pot roast beef topped with melted swiss, piled into a long bun and served with jus, but there's something about this particular thick jus and beef that's a perfect combination.

And the restaurant isn't just a drive-in, it's a diner, too. Some have compared the atmosphere to Arnold's from *Happy Days*, and I can understand that. The main body of the restaurant is one long dinette, complete with short bar and stools and red pleather booths. Coca-Cola memorabilia, 1950s décor, Elvis cut-outs and an actual honest-to-goodness Razorback Rider—you know, the sort where you put money in a mechanism and the "ride" bounces back and forth for the kid on it—complete the ensemble.

Outside Arkansas, Ed Walker's is likely known best for its five-pound burger. No joke, the largest burger in the state of Arkansas comes from right here. It's not a recent thing—you can see a very old newspaper clipping on the wall that shows one—but it is unusual. Most places that serve something that big have a competition. Well yeah, there's one here too—eat the burger and an order of fries in forty-five minutes, and the meal is yours for free—but that's only because enough people came in recently and griped that there wasn't a contest. The giant cheeseburger is sliced into eight pieces and served with a pie server. It comes out on a pizza pan and a platter of condiments to put on it. And it's meant to serve a family of six to eight people.

DINER CULTURE

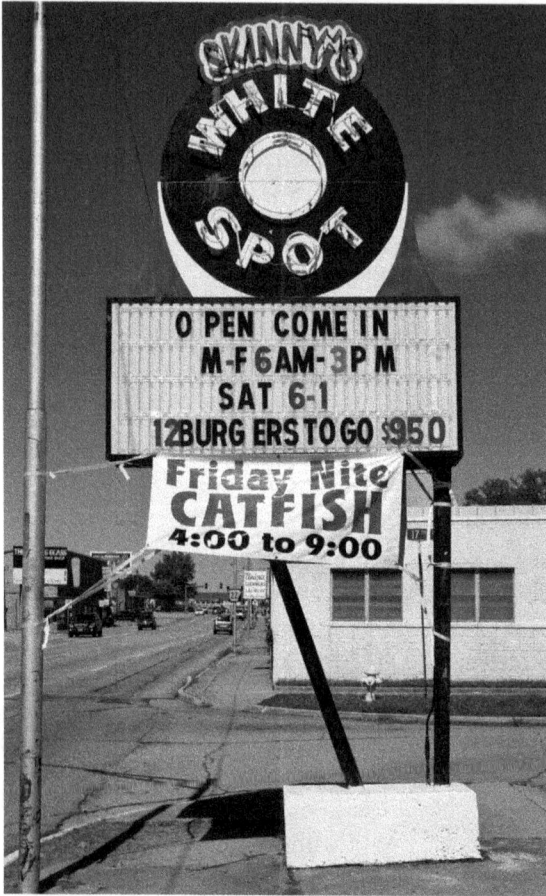

Skinny's White Spot Café in Fort Smith. *Grav Weldon.*

As I mentioned first, there's a diner culture. The city is packed with them. Several are twenty-four hours in nature, and almost all of them share the same distinctions—hearty breakfasts, plate-lunch specials and pie, all cheap and served up fast. Diners fluxed into Fort Smith to meet the demands of the highway crowd and to service the folks who worked shifts at one of the city's many manufacturing plants, which is also why they endure today.

Many of the original diners have passed into history. (This was, after all, where the first Old South Restaurant [page 121] opened its doors in the 1940s.) Of the coffee-and-a-meal places that opened post–World War II, just two remain: Ed Walker's Drive In and Skinny's White Spot Café.

Skinny's White Spot Café

First opened in 1947, the White Spot has had its share of locations. Today, it sits on the corner of Seventeenth Street and Rogers Avenue. It boasts many things, including what's likely the cheapest burger in the city, a ninety-cent wonder that's even cheaper bought in bulk. (The sign out front has recently boasted a deal of twelve burgers for $9.50). As of this writing in 2013, a bowl of beans with a side of cornbread is just over a buck.

Notice I called it the White Spot. That's because it's always been the White Spot. Back in 2008, Skinny's Catfish in Van Buren closed, and the owner purchased the Fort Smith diner. And he didn't change a thing—except, on Friday nights, Skinny's White Spot serves up some of the best fried catfish you've ever had in your life. So two historic restaurants have become one, and today, there's new neon on the old round sign.

Bob and Ellie's

In 1986, Bob and Ellie's opened up on the south side of town. A marvelous twenty-four-hour joint that focuses more on dinner than breakfast and lunch, the place has managed to survive, despite a crazy location. Though it's located on U.S. Highway 271, that route is primarily used by truckers heading to one of the area's plants. Bob and Ellie's has survived where local favorites Worldburger and Gina's Italian Beef have failed. Even today, you can get a good meal cheap there.

Benson's Grill

If you ask around town about diners, chances are you'll be referred to what's known as Fort Smith's king of late-night dining. Benson's Grill was started in 1992 by Benson "Ben" Canoy. He named the place more after his grandfather (his namesake) than himself. It quickly became the hottest twenty-four-hour ticket in town.

Benson's Grill is about comfort food. It's known for sweet potato pancakes served with a lump of margarine and a hot dispenser of syrup, for greasy patty melts and burgers, for the BELT (a BLT with egg) and the GOT'cha (Gravy On Top of eggs, biscuits, hash browns and sausage) and for the mysterious Chump (never on the menu and never revealed to those who do not choose to dine on the divine delicacy).

Canoy sold the place five years after opening to Don Tate, who still runs it today. Canoy ended up starting Lucy's Diner in 2010, naming that establishment after his mom. He passed away in February 2013.

Benson's Grill in Fort Smith. *Grav Weldon.*

Still, at Benson's there's something happening at all hours. If it's after midnight and you spot a sign on the table when you walk in, leave it alone—someone's gone out to have a cigarette. If it's dawn and the jukebox is humming, wait until Stevie Ray Vaughan is done before you drop in another quarter. And whenever you go, listen for the sweet drawl of one of the even sweeter waitresses who are full of conversation, advice and suggestions on your perfect comfort-food breakfast.

DAIRY DINERS

Ed Walker's may cross the line from drive-in to diner, but there are still plenty of drive-ins around the town. One of the oldest comes close to the joint's longevity. That'd be the DAIRY FREEZE on Midland.

Not associated with the former small-range Dairy Freeze chain in Arkansas (many locations of which still operate, though independently), the location on Midland can be traced back to the 1950s and maybe even the '40s. Even the current staff isn't certain. What are certain are the old drive-up-and-order frame, with stalls perpendicular to the driveway rather than at a diagonal, and the Frito chili pie—the best in town.

Dairy Freeze in Fort Smith. *Grav Weldon.*

Reed's Twin Burger in Fort Smith. *Grav Weldon.*

What keeps drawing folks to this drive-in, just blocks from the Arkansas River, is the nostalgia—and the butterscotch shakes. I find myself popping in every now and again to get a dipped cone—just for research purposes, of course.

If you're looking for onion rings, REED'S TWIN BURGER is a good bet. Styled as a 1950s drive-in, this little restaurant at the corner of Tulsa and Twenty-fourth Streets carries about a dozen different varieties of burgers and a half dozen different dogs, along with several side items. The area's wide ethnic palate is even addressed, with egg rolls and burritos on the menu. It's hard to believe from the look of the place that it actually opened in 1986, or so we're told. Its location near Carnall Elementary probably doesn't hurt its business.

Then there's THE YELLOW UMBRELLA. Located right off the campus of Ballman Elementary, the diminutive burger stand is sort of umbrella shaped. Open since the 1970s, the little drive-in sells burgers, shakes and sno-cones.

THE RED BARN

After World War II, Fort Smith underwent a restaurant boom. Not only did the diner scene take off, but family restaurants also became very popular. The next generation saw another explosion, with family restaurants becoming more distinctive and more ethnic.

A family sit-down at The Red Barn Steakhouse. *Grav Weldon.*

The city's oldest steakhouse is The Red Barn. Located on the north side of town off Midland, not far from the Arkansas River, this is a restaurant within a century-old barn. In fact, this particular facility was used as a farm for Tennessee Walking Horses, one of which, it's proudly shared, was purchased by Mr. J.C. Penney himself. It is an established place of horsery.

Of course, there's more to it than that. Yes, the walls are still covered in farm implements and related décor, and the tables are located in stalls. But the floor is concrete and clean, and the food is marvelous. Eschewing new fads and trends, the menu has remained relatively the same since the 1946 opening.

The star of the show is the steak: New York strips, filet mignon, prime rib, T-bone and a twenty-two-ounce porterhouse that's the restaurant's specialty. Steaks come grilled or "chef charbroiled," and they are known to be amazingly tender.

The house-made blue cheese dressing is renowned for its chunky texture. And the ham steak topped with a pineapple ring is right out of a 1960s road movie. But what I really find fascinating is the quail—as in, the pan-fried Boston Mountain quail. Here's a locally sourced bird that's always been brought in from close by, hand-battered and fried up in a cast-iron skillet. Get one or get two; the birds come with cream gravy and a baked potato. I can't think of another place that offers pan-fried quail, really.

What I hear the most about, though, are the biscuits. They come twenty to a pan, bite sized and buttery. Known as "Granny's little biscuits," they are highly addictive. Ask for yours when you order an appetizer and sneak a couple into your doggie bag, which you're probably going to need.

EMMY'S GERMAN RESTAURANT

While there are many communities in Arkansas that were started by German immigrants (Stuttgart comes to mind) and while there are many German influences on Arkansas cuisine (including fried cabbage, the slaw used on Arkansas barbecue sandwiches and the kraut on the corned beef sandwich), there are few German restaurants.

The influences do remain in other ways, such as in some of our baking and stews. And there are a few restaurants that have sparked since then. Of them, there's just one that's stood for more than fifty years. That's Emmy's German Restaurant in Fort Smith.

After World War II, Al Thome was stationed in Offenbach, Germany, a short distance south of Frankfurt. There, he met a young lady named Emmy Werner, and he married her. They lived in Offenbach for a few years, and Emmy and her mother taught Al how to cook. He learned traditional German dishes and the methods in which they came together.

After a few years, the Thomes decided to come to America. First they relocated to Illinois, where Al was from. Then they moved to Fort Smith. There, it soon became apparent that a new restaurant might not be a bad idea.

See, Fort Smith didn't have much as far as international cuisine goes. Anything past plate dinners, cafeterias, fish, burgers and doughnuts was kind of foreign to those who dined out. This was a decade before the birth of Taliano's, the Lighthouse or any of the other fine dining experiences available in the western Arkansas town.

So in 1962, Al and Emmy opened a little Bavarian-style restaurant on Eleventh Street, serving what they called wunderbarsten—or, for English speakers, the best—of German food. They moved the restaurant a short while later to Sixteenth Street, where it became Zum Deutschen Eck (The German Corner). The eatery became the place where many Arkansawyers encountered their first sauerbraten, schnitzel, spatzel and strudel.

At some point, the name on the Victorian house at 602 North Sixteenth Street changed to Emmy's German Restaurant, and for forty years, it was one of the top places for dates, proms and wedding receptions. Al even came up with a deep-fried cheese recipe that's borne up through the ages.

Served with mustard, it's an otherworldly experience.

Al and Emmy loved their restaurant, and they loved Fort Smith. But they never had any children. When they passed away, Emmy's closed—briefly.

Then the son of the owner of Taliano's—that other great place serving fine food to promgoers and wedding parties just a few blocks away—came into the picture. Joe Caldarera shared some of those fine schnitzel memories with many other Fort Smith residents. He decided to keep the love going. He approached Al's sister, who had kept ahold of the recipes that had been used at Emmy's for more than forty years. He bought them, bought the old banquet hall that Emmy's had utilized and brought back this old favorite.

Top: Al Thome. *Courtesy Joe Caldarera.*

Bottom: Emmy Thome. *Courtesy Joe Caldarera.*

CLASSIC EATERIES OF THE OZARKS AND ARKANSAS RIVER VALLEY

Today, Emmy's is still serving up Al and Emmy's delicious dishes—her famed chicken *cordon bleu*, his fried cheese and all the other odd-sounding (to American ears) German dishes. Joe has added his own, and today, you can enjoy such items as German eggrolls, red snapper fromage and vegetarian pasta.

Emmy's German Restaurant is one of just three German restaurants in the whole state. When I mentioned I was writing this book and was interested in some recipes, Joe sent along this one for the beloved potato pancakes, for which I am thankful.

POTATO PANCAKES
EMMY'S GERMAN RESTAURANT, FORT SMITH

5 large Idaho russet potatoes
1 large yellow onion
3 large eggs
1 cup buttermilk
¾ teaspoon ground nutmeg
1 tablespoon salt
1 teaspoon ground black pepper
1 tablespoon dry parsley flakes
2 cups flour
1 tablespoon butter

Peel and shred potatoes. Store shredded potatoes in a bowl of cold water.

Peel and dice the onion. Drain the potatoes and gently squeeze out some of the moisture. Add potato, onions, eggs, buttermilk and remaining spices in a mixing bowl. This will create a wet mixture.

Slowly add the flour while gently mixing all the ingredients. More or less flour may be needed depending on the consistency you prefer.

Melt butter in a large skillet or flat top grill and spoon the mixture onto the hot surface making pancake-sized circles. Cook on both sides until golden brown.

Serve with spicy mustard and honey mustard.

TALIANO'S ITALIAN RESTAURANT

Now for a history lesson of sorts—or, shall I say, a bunch of different bits of history lessons.

Taliano's Italian Restaurant resides in a two-story brick home, the 1887 J.M. Sparks Mansion. Two men opened the elegant eatery in 1970. Jim Cadelli and Tom Caldarera took the recipes their mothers taught them and put them to good use within the walls of the home, changing little over the years but the prices.

It's easily the most romantic place to dine in the city—chandeliers that have been converted from gas to electric, fleur-de-lis carpeting, velvet drapes and candlelight. Why have I not experienced the magic?

Oh, but I have. I even remember the date of my first visit: August 5, 1993. My boyfriend and I were marking six months of togetherness. I had the veal scallopini. He had the seafood diavolo. He had red wine. I had a cappuccino (a novelty to me at the time). I had an accident and spilled said beverage down the front of my shirt. He had a conniption fit. I insisted we stay for tiramisu.

Taliano's Italian Restaurant in Fort Smith. *Grav Weldon.*

For two young folks to drive up from Russellville for dinner is something else. And the incident didn't mar my love for the place. After all, the sauce was flavorful and fresh, the pasta pliant and marvelous, the cappuccino wet, the tiramisu a moist and caffeinated dream that fueled the drive home since the cappuccino couldn't.

When the restaurant opened in 1970, there weren't any other Italian restaurants in town. Today, there are several. Taliano's survives because it doesn't change. The two families still run it, with grandchildren now filling their grandparents' roles. The menu is perfect as is. The house is beautiful. It's still a popular place for wedding receptions and prom night dinners, and as long as the families stick with it, it'll remain that way.

Family-Style Dining

CATFISH COVE's advertising and Facebook argue over the start date of the restaurant. While the advertising logo states the place has been around since 1971, its Facebook page puts that start at 1974. However long the restaurant's been on, the buffet has gone on forever. Fried catfish, frog legs and shrimp are included, and on Tuesday nights (and sometimes on Saturdays), the place packs out for all-you-can-eat crab legs. If you have kids, ask to be seated near the gigantic fish tank—not only is it the brightest spot not directly under a heat lamp, but it's also fun to watch.

JERRY NEEL's has been around since 1977, first along U.S. 71 south of town and now at its current location on Phoenix Avenue. The Neel folks are from Clark County, but they've made a home in Fort Smith and are comfortable. They also make what might be the pinkest smoked beef brisket I have ever had. Pork, ham, sausage, bologna, turkey, chicken—if it's meat, they'll smoke it and serve it up. The twice-baked potato is a thing of beauty, and if it's in season, you have to get the strawberry shortcake.

Since 1982, GEORGE's RESTAURANT has been perched on Grand Avenue, a sturdy brown edifice that's consistently served up fare to the city's residents. Created by George and Alex Catsavis, this local joint offers dinner entrées, nachos and burgers and, for some reason, has a fondness for piling on big mounds of hand-cut, homemade french fries on anything within reason (and then giving you an extra plate to move them onto). It's also the oldest place in town to get a gyro; the Catsavises

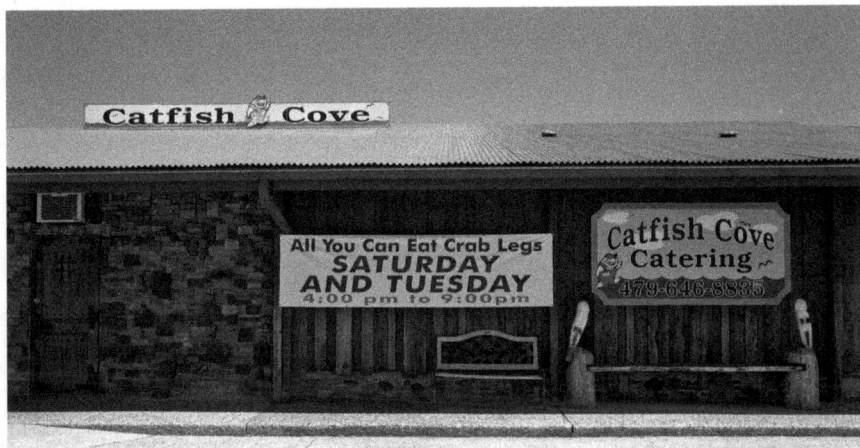

Catfish Cove in Fort Smith. *Grav Weldon.*

are of Greek ancestry. Oh, and they offer pies regularly, from cherry to chocolate peanut butter.

The oldest still-operating Chinese restaurant in the city is DIAMOND HEAD. It's had two operating locations at any one point, one on Towson and one on Midland, the second of which is still open. The egg rolls are sublime. Newcomers blown away with the eclectic menu are usually directed toward "The Bowl"—which is a big bowl of noodles in sauce with chicken and beef. And it's good, but if you believe yourself able to take the heat, you have to try Miller's Bomb Squad. Named for a guy that used to head the bomb squad for the city's police department, it's a spicy, spicy, *spicy* bowl of, well, everything. Hey, it's been good for thirty years or better.

RE-PETE'S PLACE is named for Pete Schmitz—sort of. Pete had a bar called Pete's Place that opened around 1933, but he passed on just six years later. The family owned it for sixty-some-odd years but closed it down in 1995. Re-Pete's sprouted in its place with an almost identical menu and sports bar feel. With burgers, beer and whatnot, it has all the things you want from a sports bar.

Historical photograph of Pete's Place in Fort Smith. *Courtesy Miss Anna's on Towson.*

LEWIS' FAMILY RESTAURANT

Lewis' Family Restaurant bears its own special mention. Open for more than thirty-five years (and at this Fort Smith location since 1993), it's a good home-cooking place, where the breads, the waffles, the pies—everything—are homemade. And then there's the Inferno Burger.

The low-slung little brown building sits at the corner of Zero and Highway 71 in the southern part of the city, at a rather busy intersection across from the local Walmart.

We dropped by late one Friday morning for breakfast in August 2010. Well, at least, *I* was planning to have breakfast. See, Grav had been hearing about this place, and he'd actually been and seen this thing on the menu. I'll get back to that in a moment.

Upon entering the building, we saw the day's special on a rather obnoxious-looking sandwich board. I was actually kind of interested in the breakfast special, peering out under signs that stated, "You have two choices—take it or leave it!" and a labeled mousetrap that said, "Complaint Department, Press Button for Service." My interest was piqued with something that looked seriously dangerous: the I-540 Pile-Up—corned beef hash topped with two eggs, cheddar cheese and gravy served with toast or a biscuit. I was intrigued, not startled into actually ordering the thing.

We found a booth along the east wall, under a specials board. Our waitress came over and dropped off menus and took our drink orders. The menu was of decent size. It didn't take me long to figure out I really wanted a pecan waffle, and I got mine "combo'd up" with a couple of over-medium eggs and a couple of rounds of turkey sausage.

Grav knew what he wanted from the start, though he did cursory flip through the menu. He was in it for this burger. It was listed on an insert page in the menu:

Inferno Burger
⅓-lb. seasoned burger topped with spicy bacon, Pepper Jack cheese, jalapenos and onions. All this on a hamburger bun smothered in Lewis' own HOT chipotle mayo. This burger is not for wimps!
$6.99 with (1) side.

He ordered his with Cajun fries. I guess that made a lot of sense.

It was loud inside. People were crowded into ad-covered tables and booths along the walls. Right next to our booth was a series of tables that had been pushed together. Guys were gathering along its length—all guys, in fact. Our waitress breezed by.

"I got your order in just in time," she told us.

"Everything okay?" I asked.

"Oh, it's the Inferno Club guys. There's a lot of them, and it's going to take a while to get their orders out. Yours should be ready in no time."

I looked at Grav, and we both looked over at the table. The guys that were filing in were greeting each other affectionately. They came from all walks of life—gentlemen in golf shirts, a guy in fatigues, some in T-shirts and a couple of boys, too. You could hear their greetings over the loud and persistent hum of conversation throughout the place. Our waitress swung back by to refill our drinks.

"Excuse me, ma'am, did you say a club?" Grav asked.

"It's a club for people who have finished the Inferno Burger. We were just offering it for a short time. But they keep coming back, and we keep leaving it on the menu."

"You have to finish the burger?" I asked.

"If you finish it, you can sit at their table. They have a Facebook page."

Now, there was a story. I raised my eyebrows at Grav. "You may not know what you're in for."

"I can take it," he confidently told me. He told me about an experience at an Indian restaurant in London, where he'd managed to eat the hottest thing they brought out of the kitchen. I just smiled.

It was loud in the restaurant and warm, too. With the temperature pushing one hundred already and all the people coming through the door, it was no wonder.

I heard a younger man over at the Inferno Club table talking about why he was there to eat the burger. He told the guys he was getting married soon and that he needed to eat the burger to prove himself. There was some chortling among other guys at the table.

"You know, I'd give it a shot, just for the hell of it, if I wasn't having this waffle this morning," I told Grav.

"You know it has bacon on it."

"Does it? Well, damn."

I looked up and saw our waitress making her way between the tables with our order. She plunked down my waffle and a separate plate with eggs and turkey sausage and then spun around the plate with the famed burger on it right in front of Grav.

"You sure about this, hon? Need any ketchup?"

"I'll take barbecue sauce if you have it," he told her, picking up his camera. She looked at us a little funny, but that wasn't going to stop us. We both started to shoot the food.

Just seconds after I had taken a whiff of the waffle my eyes watered a little bit.

"Is that the burger?"

"I think so."

"Wow. Do you want to shoot the waffle?"

"Yes, yes, I do." We traded plates. I noticed how the bun was hunched over the contents of the burger, so I just barely brushed it back before I started to shoot. The scent of strong peppers and onions was close to overwhelming. But it looked like a really great thing to eat. I looked back at my waffle and sighed a little. I had to get that waffle. It was part of my own assignment. (At the time, I was working on a breakfast-related cover story for the *Arkansas Times*.)

We traded back plates, and I shot some of the eggs. I was startled by Grav's sudden exclamation.

"Good Lord!"

"You haven't eaten it yet," I said.

"I just took a bite." He took a big gulp of his Mountain Dew. "It's really hard to handle." I turned my camera back on and pointed it his way. He tackled the burger with fork and knife. "Look at this bacon. This is nothing but spice."

"Hotter than you thought?"

"Maybe."

I started to cut a little piece of my waffle, but before I could get it to my lips, I saw him fork up a chunk of burger. I put down my fork and took a shot of him. Then, I watched as he ate it.

"Wow. Holy shit." He had suddenly beaded up with sweat, and his pallor had changed from light pink to a deepening red. He was chuckling a little bit. I watched as he took off his glasses and wiped his face with a napkin.

My waffle was all but forgotten. I was just astounded by what I was seeing before me, this transformation of willpower into pain, and I had to capture each moment of it. I started scribbling his utterances in my notebook. This was going to be good.

He cut another bite. "Aw! One of the hottest things I've ever eaten," he told me. He stopped, looked at me and asked, "What have I done to myself?"

I looked over at the guys at the other table. No one had an Inferno Burger yet. I looked back and just grinned. He continued his monologue

Grav faces the Inferno Burger Challenge. *Kat Robinson.*

as I scribbled. "I like hot food, but that being said, I can feel it coming out of my sinuses." He picked up and ate a Cajun spiced fry with no visual change. Then back to the burger. I noticed he was taking smaller and smaller bites.

"So, what's in it?"

"The stuff they call mayo is the source of the heat. There's spice in the meat, too." He coughed hard. "Ooh, spice up the nose, wild."

"The cheese?"

"There's cheese? Oh, yeah, there is." He wiped his face again with the napkin, dabbing around his eyes. Sweat had rolled down his chest and he was squinting a bit. He called the waitress. "Ma'am, I could use a cup of milk."

"Do you want us to add it to the check?" she asked me. I waved my hand and nodded.

"Whole milk if you got it!" he hollered as best as he could, trying not to choke up.

She came back a fraction of a minute later. "We only have 2 percent."

"Yes! I need it!"

His plummet into deeper shades of red hadn't stopped when he stopped taking in bites of burger. In fact, the heat had stirred up a fountain within his skin, dampening his shirt one degree after another, as if to attempt to save him from the inferno by drowning him.

"This is on par with 'we can make it hotter.' This is insane hot."

Our waitress brought the milk, and Grav took it and took a long drink. He leaned over for a moment, trying for a little air I think. I took the opportunity to put down my camera and try my breakfast.

It wasn't cold, which means it was pretty hot when I got it. The eggs were perfectly cooked, but the turkey sausage lacked spice. The waffle, on the other hand, was excellent, a big Belgian with pecans throughout, light yet golden and crispy and a sponge for butter and syrup.

"I'm usually not a milk drinker," Grav gasped, finally able to speak. "It just keeps building and building." He fiddled with his fork but didn't progress on to the next bite.

I got a little syrup on my fingers and did the unconscious thing, which was to lick it off. Suddenly my lips were on fire. "The heck?"

"You all right?"

"I think I must have touched your burger. Wow. That's some spice." I wiped my hands against the napkin and made a note that I needed to go wash them as soon as I was done eating.

The guys at the next table were getting their food. I could hear some general fun being poked at one of the guys who'd ordered a big salad instead of the burger. He good naturedly took the chiding.

Grav put down his napkin. "I'm done. I swear, I taste ghost chilies in there."

"Are you sure? You haven't even made it halfway through."

"I could eat the whole thing if I tried. But I have a shoot today, and I don't want to miss it. I could take some Pepsid and make it work…"

I was enjoying the waffle and watching the entertainment in front of me. I really did feel for Grav as far as the heat was concerned, but he had put himself through it.

"I'm feeling a mild to moderate amount of miserable," he continued, taking another drink from his large tumbler of milk. "I want to take another bite—it tastes good—but it's so hot not just in my mouth but on my lips and the inside of my nose."

He asked for a box and took just the burger with him, having not made much of a dent in the fries. I got up and settled our check.

When I got home, I checked Facebook for the page I'd heard about. It's a private page, and when I requested membership, I got a message from Brad Lewis asking if I'd actually eaten the burger. I explained the situation, and he sent me this reply:

> We were wondering who that was taking pictures of us! The Inferno Club started when I was telling one guy at my church about the burger. Another guy overheard, then another. So we decided to meet at Lewis' to eat it. We enjoyed the food and the fellowship so much we decided to make it a monthly get-together and invite anyone to down the burger. They've made a special "Inferno" menu for us now. A person has to eat the entire burger to join the club but doesn't have to eat it every time we meet. I've eaten seven of them, and two members have eaten the Towering Inferno (double all) and have decided to retire from Inferno anything.

Grav and I both posted photos on our Facebook pages after his ordeal, and we got a lot of comments. In fact, there are several of our friends who are being very macho about it, who want to try it and see if they can manage it. I am going nowhere near that burger, except to capture my friends' agony as they attempt to eat it.

And Grav, that son of a gun, kept going. He took the rest of the burger home and ate the rest of it over three days, usually posting to Facebook and griping each time. But he did it. The Inferno Club even took him at his word.

I still have yet to hear of a hotter burger.

CALICO COUNTY

For two years, every time I would leave Fort Smith and the place was open, I'd go by Calico County to pick up a box of day-old cinnamon rolls. Some days, they wouldn't have any, and I'd pony up for the fresh ones instead. I'd have to put them in the back of the vehicle so I wouldn't eat them on the drive back to Little Rock.

That Calico County stop was the last thing I'd do before I left town, so it seems fitting it's the last stop I'm going to take you on before I head out to other places in Arkansas in this book.

It opened in 1984, a quaint memorabilia-bespeckled eatery a block off Rogers Avenue. Every wall was taken up with historic photographs of Fort Smith's famed landmarks, cola signs, knickknacks and the like. The LaRoche family who started the restaurant filled the place wall to wall with pieces of Fort Smith, from old grocery store signs to ancient toys. The space was packed with booths and tables, and those, in turn, were always packed with folks.

They come for the food—generous portions, hometown favorites and crazy things, too, like deep-fried corn on the cob and battered and deep-fried ribs. Chris Chamberlain named the restaurant in his book *The Southern Foodie: 100 Places to Eat in the South Before You Die* and for good reason—the fat menu's packed with home-cooking favorites. Oprah Winfrey walked in one day in 2006. The whole cast of *Biloxi Blues*—including Matthew Broderick and Jennifer Gray—dined there in 1988.

And those cinnamon rolls—unlike the average cinnamon roll—aren't caked or iced with way too much sugar. They're traditional, little home-style rolls full of cinnamon, tightly rolled and sliced and baked. And when you sit down, the waitress brings you out a towel-lined basket with a couple. To me, on a normal day, that single warm-from-the-oven cinnamon roll and a cup o' joe would be enough for breakfast. There's a counter on the website that marks how many of those cinnamon rolls have been served—over six million of the coffee-perfect rolls.

That counter, though, stopped on November 26, 2012, when a fire started in the kitchen. Though the structure stood after the flames were out, all those pieces of Fort Smith that had decked the walls were soaked and stained with smoke. The restaurant was closed.

Current owners Larry LaRoche and Scott Blair never thought of closing for good. Within forty-eight hours, they were able to share some good news with their employees—insurance was going to take care of things, and until the repairs were completed, everyone was going to get paid.

Inside Calico County before the fire. *Grav Weldon.*

As I write this, in July 2013, I have a message in my inbox. It's a good message. It says Calico County will be reopening in a manner of weeks and that every diner will be greeted with that same basket of hot cinnamon rolls wrapped in a patch of calico. And every time I look at that message, I drool.

The recipe for those cinnamon rolls is a secret, but the Calico County folks were gracious enough to share another of my favorites from their menu.

SQUASH CASSEROLE
CALICO COUNTY, FORT SMITH

6 medium yellow crookneck squash
I small yellow onion, finely chopped
⅔ stick margarine, softened
2 tablespoons sugar
2 teaspoons salt
I teaspoon black pepper
2 eggs
I¾ cups cornbread crumbs
I cup evaporated milk
I¼ cups finely shredded cheddar cheese

Preheat oven to 375 degrees.

Boil squash. When soft, mash with a potato masher in a colander and let drain for 10 minutes.

In a large mixing bowl, add all ingredients except cheese and mix thoroughly (best done with a tabletop mixer with paddle attachment).

Pour into a greased 8 by 12 Pyrex glass dish and bake for 35 minutes. Add cheese to top and bake an additional 10 minutes.

Chapter 5

DUAL ROUTES OF THE ARKANSAS RIVER VALLEY

T he Massey Motor Court in Fort Smith, like so many of the other lodging properties in the city, put out postcards in the heyday of the motorist. Massey's stood out, though, for the addition of a convenient map that showed how Arkansas Highway 22 (the Little Rock Highway) was a quicker route to the east than U.S. 64. Of course, being on Highway 22, it had reason to be biased in that direction.

However, the map itself is of intrigue and interest, showing how the communities on either side of the Arkansas River were aligned and how Dardanelle was the great crossover point. It, of course, excludes I-40, which wasn't built through that section of Arkansas until the 1960s. Classic restaurants dot the landscape on both sides of the river, more so on the north side, simply from the traffic generated from interstate travelers.

Let's start with Arkansas Highway 22, on the south side of the river. It starts out as Rogers Avenue, coming directly southeast out of downtown Fort Smith and passing Fort Chaffee at Barling. Highway 22 will get you pretty much right to Paris and then to Dardanelle, a nice scenic route with plenty to see.

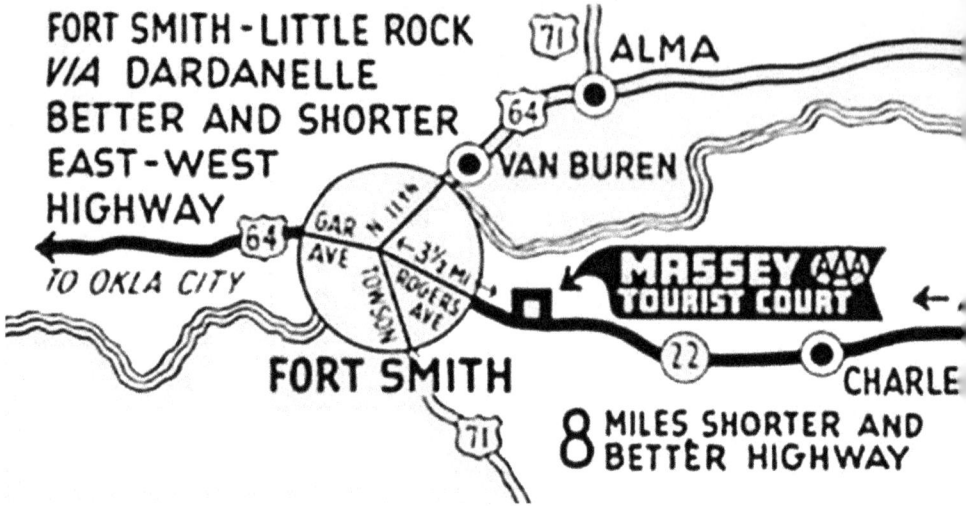

Map from the Massey Motor Court historic postcard.

ARKANSAS HIGHWAY 22 FROM BARLING TO DARDANELLE

Bruce Terri Drive-In

The name Bruce Terri Drive-In may sound odd, but it's not, in fact, a single person's name. It's a combined name from Bill and Peggy Shopfner's children.

The Shopfners' restaurant days go back to 1961, when the couple purchased the Frostee across from where Central Mall went in on Rogers Avenue in Fort Smith. When the announcement was made that Rogers was going to be widened for all that mall traffic, they decided to relocate way down the road, where it's just Highway 22 in the town of Barling. They renamed it to Bruce Terri after their son and daughter and set up shop.

In 1987, Terri bought the place from her parents. Today, she and her husband, Chuck Peacock, run the place, and that's why there's a peacock on the sign. They also started up a catering business that year, and it's very popular—so popular that even Governor Mike Beebe has called for their services. The business has a giant catering trailer and a small fleet of towable grills to boot.

98

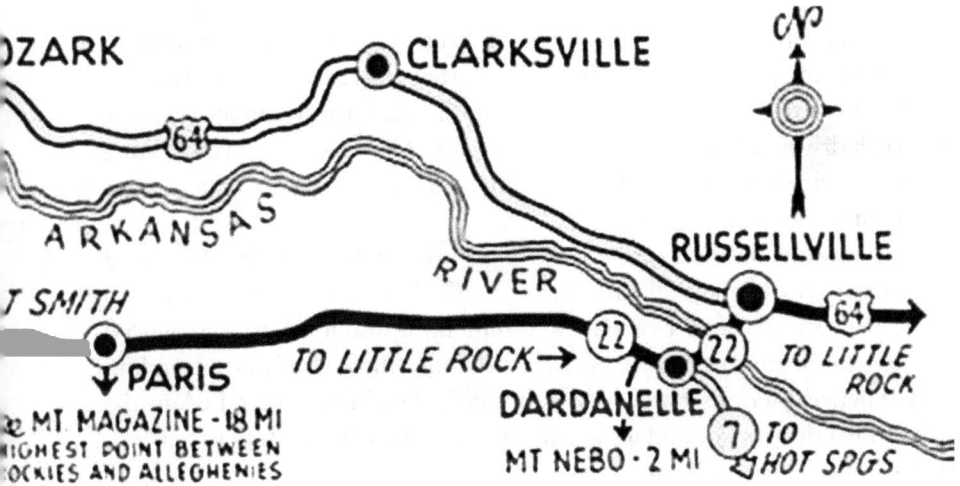

On the menu are smokehouse-style barbecue, catfish and half-pound giant hamburgers and cheeseburgers. Chili-cheese burritos and spaghetti sometimes pop up on the specials board. My best advice: whatever you get, pick up a chocolate shake.

Today, Chuck and Terri's sons, Kyrk and Chip, work alongside their parents. Chip's married now to Randie, and their daughter, Maggie, steps in as well, making this catering and drive-in operation a four-generation tradition.

Steffey's Pizza

Then there is Steffey's. It's located in Lavaca, which is out past Barling and not really close to anywhere. But you have to go. It quite possibly could be the best pizza in the state of Arkansas.

I don't say that lightly. I love Za Za and Iriana's and Rod's and Tommy's, but this is different. And maybe, it's more this one special pizza. The pie in question is the Uncle Roman, a double-crusted stuffed pie baked in a twelve-inch cast-iron skillet. It may not have been around as long as the restaurant has, but it's made its mark with me.

Back in the 1950s, Glen Steffey was stationed at Fort Chaffee, where he was assigned the position of baker. Between Fort Smith and Delmont,

Pennsylvania, he developed his very own crust and sauce recipes, and he opened the first Steffey's with his wife, Ruth, there in 1963. After a few years, she decided to be a stay-at-home mom, and he decided to pursue a career as a truck driver. They shut the place down, but Glen really enjoyed making pizza, and within a few years, they were making and selling pizza out of their basement a couple of nights a week.

The trucking business started slowing down in the area in 1980, and Glen went to Stiegler, Oklahoma, to work. One day, he went over to Lavaca to visit his friend Don Ray, and something about the area convinced him he was meant to be there. So he moved the whole family down and, in 1981, opened Steffey's Pizza. Glen eventually taught daughter LeAnn the recipes he'd developed, and today, she operates the place with her husband, Shayne, and daughter Briar.

Steffey's Pizza started out in a location west of the current store before being moved downtown, where it thrived for a couple decades. The new store opened in 2008. It's clean and homey with four big pizza ovens exposed in the kitchen that's right in front of you when you walk in the door. There's a game room with a pool table, an old-fashioned Horwitzer jukebox (that plays for free) and arcade to the left and a dining room featuring tables lit with lights ensconced in cheese graters to the right.

There are many pizzas available at Steffey's with all sorts of toppings. There are sandwiches—big sub sandwiches baked in the ovens. There are nachos and breadsticks and salads. But all these pale compared to that one specially featured pie in the middle of the menu.

The Uncle Roman hasn't always been on the menu—it was something that was put out on the buffet early in the week on Monday through Wednesday that caught on. Because it takes an extra fifteen minutes to cook, the folks who run the restaurant were afraid it wouldn't catch on. But people are understanding when they see that direction on the menu to expect a longer cook time. There's just one size for the Uncle Roman, and you choose the toppings.

Steffey's crust is different—a flatbread sort instead of the cracker crust you get at so many Arkansas locations. And the sauces aren't limited to marinara—mustard, barbecue, ranch dressing and olive oil are also offered.

LeAnn was gracious enough to share the recipe for the Uncle Roman.

UNCLE ROMAN
STEFFEY'S PIZZA, LAVACA

18 ounces pizza dough (you'll have to come up with
your own—Steffey's is a secret), divided into 10- and
8-ounce pieces
6 ounces pizza sauce
(you'll have to come up with that, too), divided
12 ounces smoked provolone cheese, divided
Your favorite pizza toppings
Garlic butter to brush on
Parmesan cheese

Preheat oven to 400 degrees. Grease bottom and sides of a 10-inch cast-iron skillet.

Roll out the 10-ounce dough ball and place in bottom of skillet. Press dough all the way up the sides of the skillet.

Spread four ounces of your favorite pizza sauce on the bottom, and then layer six ounces of the cheese on that. Add your favorite toppings generously, and then top with the remaining six ounces of provolone and two ounces of pizza sauce.

Roll out the eight-ounce dough ball and place on top of skillet. Pinch dough edges together as you would a deep-dish pie and brush with garlic butter. Sprinkle Parmesan cheese over the top. Cut vent holes.

Bake at 400 degrees for 30 minutes until golden brown.

Rolling Down Arkansas Highway 22

There are other restaurants along the way. At Charleston, you'll find a DAIRY DINER that dates back to 1989. Then, at Paris, there's ROGER'S DAIRY CREAM that goes back to 1985. There's the DAIRY DE-LITE, originally opened in 1988 as part of the famed chain. It's gone through a few owners but, in 2013, opened under new management.

And then there's THE GRAPEVINE RESTAURANT. It was started in 1991 by two people from California—sort of. See, Kenneth Vines's folks moved to Arkansas when he was four. His wife, Lisa, moved here when she was

The Grapevine Restaurant in Paris. *Kat Robinson.*

eleven. They grew up in Paris together and were high school sweethearts. They married in 1976.

They tried life in Kansas City. But the big-city life wasn't for them, so they came back home. Over two decades, the couple would try just about every job in town, while raising a family of six children. Then, in 1990, Kenneth mentioned to sister Linda the idea of reviving the old 22 Café on U.S. 64. She thought he was nuts, but after a few months, it no longer sounded like such a crazy idea. A year later, in February 1991, The Grapevine Restaurant opened its doors.

It's a great little home-cooking restaurant with a legendary taco salad and house-smoked meats on the menu. But what truly sets the place apart is the bread. The soft, wheaty homemade bread is served to every customer with honey butter, and I swear, I could make a meal on it.

Past Subiaco, you come to New Blaine, and in that small community, you'll find a place called the DINNER BUCKET. The name might not be the most appetizing, but the food sure is. Since the place opened in 1985, it's become well known for its hand-battered chicken-fried steak and for the jellies and jams served up front. It also includes a massive pie cooler up front, full of different varieties like coconut cream, lemon icebox and (in season) fresh strawberry pie.

Highway 22 continues on through Delaware before meeting Scenic Highway 7 in Dardanelle, where we'll pick up in the next chapter.

U.S. 64 FROM VAN BUREN TO LONDON

The WPA Guide to 1930s Arkansas described U.S. 64 thusly:

> *The most direct route across the middle of Arkansas. From the Delta it runs*
> *directly west to intersect U.S. 67, which it follows southwest for some 30*
> *miles. It then turns west again, reaches the Arkansas River near Conway,*
> *and follows the northern valley wall to Fort Smith…Between Conway and*
> *Fort Smith U.S. 64 runs along the north valley wall of the Arkansas River,*
> *a natural westward path that was used for centuries by Indians and white*
> *hunters and trappers before the first trading towns sprang up along it and*
> *steamboats began to ascend the river.*

While there's little denying that hotel postcard showing the mileage difference between Fort Smith and Russellville, there's also no denying that U.S. 64 was the most direct route across Arkansas until I-40 came through, and then, it was just a matter of convenience and speed.

The highway's significance may not be as famous as Route 66, but for generations of travelers, it was the major east–west corridor across Arkansas, especially for those travelers coming from Memphis. On its western end, it crosses the Arkansas River in downtown Fort Smith on what used to be called the Free Bridge. Heading out from there, it runs concurrent with U.S. 71B over the river again, through Van Buren and back to Alma, and then it heads on its own through the River Valley, paralleling Interstate 40. At Conway, it veers due east, crossing to U.S. 67 (these days an interstate-quality highway), and then zigzags north to Bald Knob, from which it makes a beeline for Marion before joining I-55 and crossing the Mississippi at West Memphis.

Before 1925, it was known as Highway A-1.

Paul's Bakery

Right over the U.S. 64/Midland Boulevard Bridge from Fort Smith, you'll find Van Buren. Just past the curve that brings downtown traffic onto U.S. 64 eastbound, you'll find an old bakery on the right.

Paul Lehnen lived in the area almost his entire life. He was born in Fort Smith, and when he was in high school and it wasn't football season, he'd work at a little doughnut shop in town. He graduated in 1952 and joined the army after a brief stint working with his sister at Roger's Bakery on

Paul's Bakery in Van Buren. *Grav Weldon.*

Jenny Lind Avenue. He was stationed in Germany and, while there, took the opportunity to travel Europe. He returned to Fort Smith in October 1958, was discharged from service at Camp Chaffee and met his future wife, Jo Ann, on the same day. They were married in September 1959.

In February of that year, Paul bought the old Mace's Bakery in downtown Van Buren. Renamed Paul's Bakery, he set about building a business that could stand the test of time. He hired mostly young folks who lived in the area, kids who would go on to be some of his best customers.

His goal was to have "an elaborate doughnut shop," and he succeeded. Over half a century and through four different moves and three generations of family, the business grew from just three employees to more than twenty.

"Mr. Paul" got up every single morning—except holidays—in the wee hours to head in and make the doughnuts, even into his seventies.

Paul Lehnen passed away in June 2012. The bakery was closed for a short time, but then, one morning, the light was back on. And the business Paul built continues on.

Craig's Family Bakery

Up at the top of the hill above downtown Van Buren, you'll find a former convenience store that smells fantastic. This is Craig's Family Bakery.

Take away the family aspect and everything else, and let's talk doughnuts. This bakery serves up a particular doughnut that would be enough for

Craig's Family Bakery in Van Buren. *Grav Weldon.*

anyone: the state's largest. The giant doughnut is roughly ten inches in diameter. Seriously, I kid you not.

The baked goods at Craig's Family Bakery are pretty good as it is, but it's crazy items like that big doughnut that get people talking. They also do a twelve-inch cruller. Miniature pastries are also popular, perfect for just a taste.

Brothers Cottage Café

The Cottage Café has been a staple at the top of the downtown hill in Van Buren since 1925. It's located across the street from the depot, where you can still catch the Arkansas and Missouri Railway excursion train to Springdale. A few years back, the place was on a downhill slide, but it's recently been purchased by John and Danny Ray, two brothers who have renamed it Brothers Country Café (fitting, since Sister's Gourmet Bistro is catty-corner down the road).

The menu's been preserved, and one of the original bakers has been rehired. The place is well known for good country dinners, big breakfasts and a mean Reuben sandwich. The Rays are also attempting to get themselves on the pie map, with their version of the mile-high meringue pie. They're doing a good job of that, too.

Kopper Kettle Smokehouse

If you head out U.S. 64 toward Alma, you'll end up passing by Kopper Kettle Candies (which we talked about on pages 63–66). You might miss what's right next door, and if you like bacon, that's a shame.

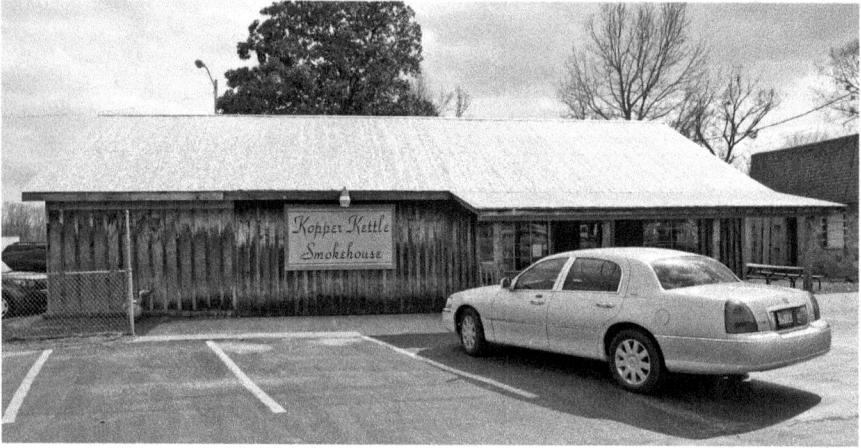

Kopper Kettle Smokehouse in Van Buren. *Grav Weldon.*

It's the Kopper Kettle Smokehouse, run by the Greer family and famed for a single item. Yes, they do amazing smoked meats, but the place has become best known for its one-pound BLT. That's not a mistake. The restaurant's folks dreamed up a perfect way to showcase their excellently smoked bacon. They serve up a full pound on a big flat bun with lettuce and tomato, and you get a to-go box when you order it. It's meant for a crowd—or a coronary.

What's often overlooked are the pies. Heck, even I have overlooked the pies. I didn't even know they had pies until recently, when Grav brought a little Styrofoam box to Little Rock. The contents: one slice of Japanese fruit pie, an amazing morsel of uniqueness I have found no place else.

Catfish Hole

Since 1993, Catfish Hole has been serving up crisp-crust catfish to travelers and locals in Alma. The place was purchased by Pat and Janie Gazzola that year. The Gazzolas, who had worked twenty-four years in the oil and gas industry, were ready for a change. Within a few years, they had expanded to Fayetteville.

Recently, a modern facility has been constructed just north of I-40 for the Catfish Hole in Alma. But it's still a great place for catfish steaks and filets served up with coleslaw, hush puppies, pickles, onions and pickle relish.

Dairy Dip

Further east in Mulberry, you'll find the Dairy Dip. It's served the community for years from a little red and white building along U.S. 64.

However, back in 2010 the place went up for sale. That's when Nathan Hunter stepped in. The twenty-five-year-old reopened the joint with Lacey Ray, whom he married the next year. Today, the restaurant is the hub of the community.

There are a lot of great things on the menu. The signature burger is known as the Big M. The sausage gravy and biscuit are well known, as are the hand-breaded onion rings. But if you want a really neat item to enjoy on your Highway 22 excursion, drop in and order a fried Snickers bar.

Rolling Down U.S. 64

Down the road in Ozark, you'll find another Dairy De-Lite (this outlet open since 1986) and ZACK'S PLACE, a pizzeria that serves up a lot more. Zack's opened in 1988 as a pizza parlor but quickly added burgers and catfish to the menu. It's also pretty well known with the locals for serving up hot chocolate chip cookies.

There's also RIVERTOWNE BBQ. It opened in 2000 and therefore doesn't quite qualify as a classic yet, though I'm sure it eventually will.

Kelt's Pub

Altus is the next town, the little burg at the heart of Arkansas Wine Country. This is certainly a place where everyone knows everyone else, and if you want a pint rather than a glass of wine, you head to Kelt's Pub.

From the side, it's a metal building. From the front, it's a little more promising. But once you're inside, you're transported elsewhere. Kelt's could be the best pub in the entire state of Arkansas, not because of some vast beer menu or trendy offering but because the whole place transports you to another country.

I've been heading to Kelt's for eighteen years now, since I graduated from Arkansas Tech. It was a favorite place for myself and my ex-husband, and it has remained a good place for me. Dan and Jan McMillan have been creating an atmosphere of comfort for years. There's nothing really fancy about the tables or the mismatched dinnerware, and that's just fine.

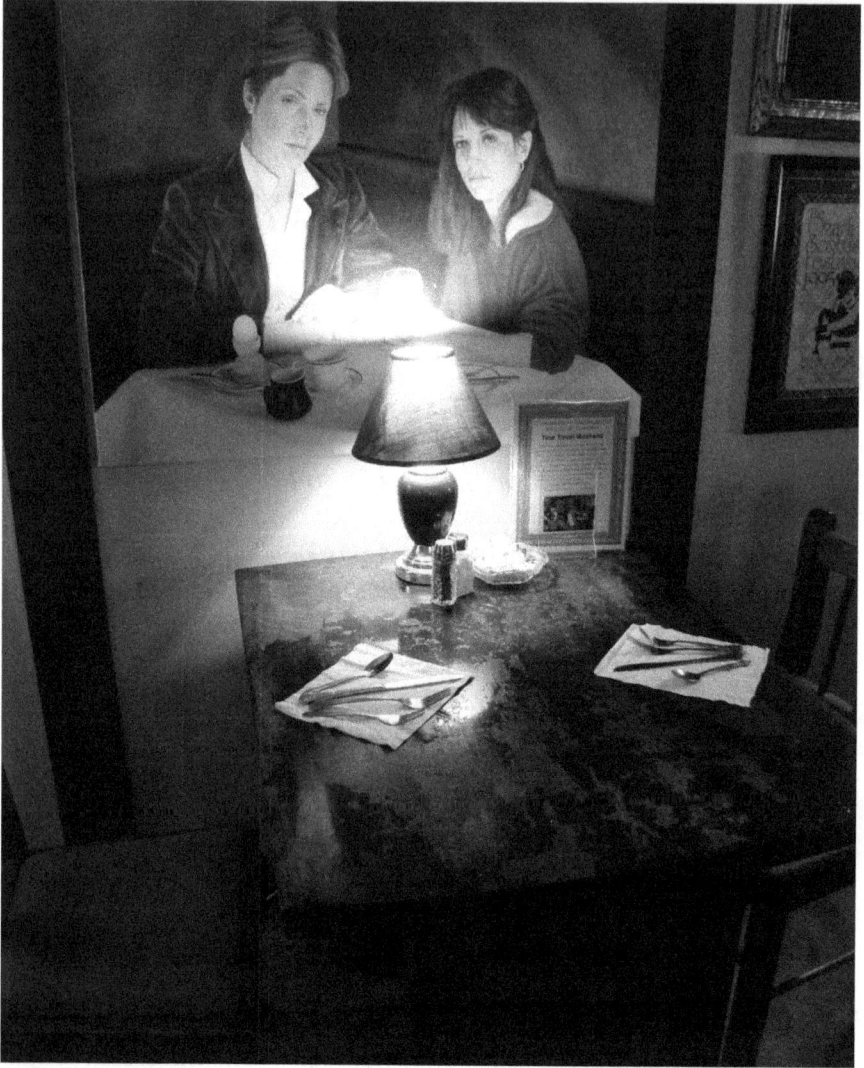

This table under the painting is considered to be the most romantic table at Kelt's Pub in Altus. *Kat Robinson*.

The McMillans are always there. I mean, Kelt's is open seven days a week, and there are few things that will cause a closure—it takes a lot of snowfall. The McMillans also have a horse farm, so that keeps them planted in Altus.

The corned beef is of legend, soaked in its brine right there, with a nice roughed texture and served up with peppercorns. The bangers and mash is spot on, but my favorite dinner is the steak: a fine rib-eye that Dan selects himself, lightly seasoned and cooked to order. It's served with a trio of condiments: a beefy jus, a light garlic butter and a creamy, slightly sweet béarnaise. Pair them with a salad with homemade blue cheese dressing and a loaf of soft, sweet bread and butter, and you have a fine and satisfying meal.

If you happen through the door with your beau or sweetheart and Jan takes a liking to you, there's a possibility you'll end up under the Lovers Portrait. This is a big painting of a couple seated at a table that hangs on the far wall of the pub.

Each December, Jan and Dan present a series of novelty dinners. They've done a medieval feast a few times, and over the past few years, they have gone to a "Dickens Dinner," where dishes from Victorian times are served up with *A Christmas Carol*, jokes and games.

One of their signature drinks was provided by the McMillans.

CHAMPAGNE MAGNOLIA
KELT'S PUB, ALTUS

Start by polishing your favorite large and elegant glass. Big wine glasses with lots of room for this celebratory summer drink work well.

5 ounces favorite Champagne
5 ounces no-pulp orange juice
2 ounces half-and-half
¼ teaspoon angostura bitters

Combine ingredients in the order given, right in the glass. Stir carefully to blend until there's a light froth on top.

Jan says, "Enjoy anytime, especially nice on Sunday afternoons, after the breakfast dishes are done and it's your turn to read the comic section of the paper."

ARKANSAS WINE COUNTRY

Altus, as I mentioned, is the heart of Arkansas wine country. It's in this tiny fragment of Ozark land that the oldest and largest wine industry in the South got started back in the nineteenth century. And it started for many of the same reasons the classic restaurants sprouted up and hung on: transportation.

In this case, railroads sparked a new population of immigrants from Germany, Switzerland and Italy that came to this region of the River Valley. The Little Rock and Fort Smith Railroad Company built its depot and freight yard in Argenta (now a district of North Little Rock) and started laying rail bed off the north banks of the Arkansas River back in 1869. Within two years some eighty miles had been run, but a railroad strike by unpaid workers brought everything to a halt, thanks to bond defaults and presumably corrupt politicians. The line was purchased by investors who changed the name to the Little Rock and Fort Smith Railway in 1875. The new investors hired German and German-speaking Swiss immigrants who set in their labor in exchange for land grants along the rail path, and that land in Franklin County eventually became the birthplace of a fledgling wine industry. (The LR&FS reached Sebastian County and Fort Smith in 1879.) It also sparked a boom in immigration for the countrymen of those first rail laborers.

Of these immigrants, two started wineries that still stand today, both in 1880. There have been many arguments over the years over who really has the claim of being first. It seems to have settled out, though, that Johann Andreas Wiederkehr and his family emigrated from Switzerland that year to Altus (the Latin word for high, exalted or profound). Wiederkehr chose land atop and to the north of St. Mary's Mountain because the area's mountains, valleys and ridges bore some resemblance to the grape-growing climates in Europe's finest wine regions. One of the things he did that first year was dig a wine cellar. We'll get back to that.

Jacob and Anna Post also came to Altus in the 1880s and started making wine there. They eventually settled on the farm of Joseph Bachman, a Swiss man who turned to viticulture when he came to the town. Bachman later became known for developing several grape varieties that are still in production today.

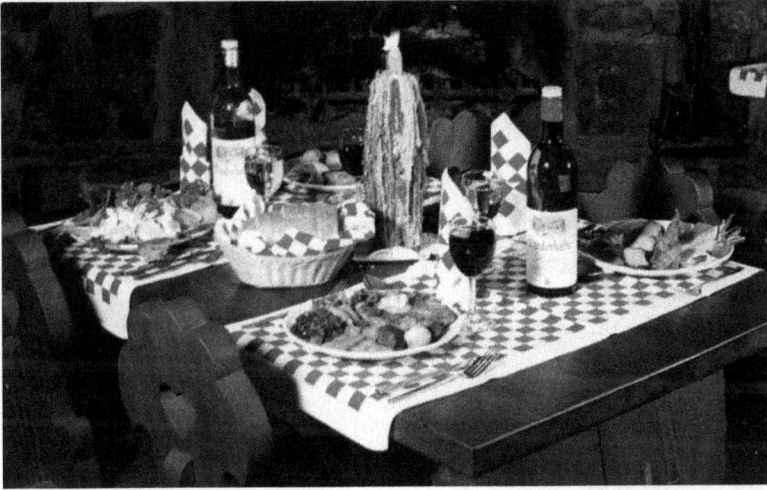

A fine dining scene at Wiederkehr Weinkeller in the 1960s. *From historic postcard.*

The Posts made wine from both wild grapes and the new varieties. During Prohibition, their daughter-in-law Katherine (married to Joseph) was sent to jail for making wine. After the ban was lifted, the Posts joined into a cooperative, which Jacob purchased in 1951 and renamed Post Winery. He continued to work with his family there until his death in an accident, when son Matt took over. Matt and his wife, Betty, had twelve children, many of whom went on to work in the winery. Today, their kids and grandkids run Post Familie Winery.

A post–World War II boom saw wineries pop up all over Arkansas, but a combination of high taxes, dry county declarations and such saw most of them fail. Just a handful survived through the twentieth century: Mount Bethel, run by Eugene and Peggy Post, started in 1956; Chateaux Aux Arc, run by Audrey House, started in 1998; and across the river in Paris, Cowie Winery, run by by Bob Cowie, started in 1967.

Over the past decade, there's been a boom in wineries in other areas of the state, with Keel's Creek in Eureka Springs (2006), Raimondo Winery in Gamaliel (2008), Tontitown Winery in Tontitown (2010, the first there since Prohibition) and Railway Winery also in Eureka Springs (2012). There's even an upstart called Movie House Winery in Morrilton that's developing products as of this writing.

WIEDERKEHR WEINKELLER RESTAURANT

But coming back to Johann Wiederkehr, that wine cellar he dug back in 1880 could be considered the oldest structure functioning as a restaurant in the River Valley today. In 1967, the family converted it into the Weinkeller Restaurant, opening the doors for fine dining in the old cellar. The cuisine has changed little. It includes Swiss-style fondue, schnitzel, steaks, chicken, Italian-style pasta and strudel, all ready to be accompanied by the Wiederkehr wines. The restaurant is open every day—except Thanksgiving, Christmas, New Year's and Easter—and welcomes thousands every year.

Wiederkehr Weinkeller Restaurant at Wiederkehr Village. *Kat Robinson*.

Rolling East Along U.S. 64

Going east along U.S. 64, you'll pass by Coal Hill's signature restaurant, DEE'S DRIVE-IN. The little beige building is full of high school memorabilia and serves a burger called the Leroy.

Diamond Drive-In in Clarksville. *Kat Robinson.*

Heading into Clarksville, you cross over I-40 and into town. It has its own Dairy Freeze that's been open since 1990, right across from the town's classic dairy diner. The DIAMOND DRIVE-IN has been around since the 1950s, and my friend Kerry Kraus can actually remember going there as a child. It's been around so long that no one at the restaurant has been able to tell me the exact year the place opened.

The Diamond Drive-In offers the usual items as at all dairy diners: fries, shakes, burgers and sodas. It also does catfish, roast beef sandwiches and fried green tomatoes. Its signature item is the WOW Burger, an oversized American cheese–laden burger, dolloped with mustard and served with a dill pickle.

From Clarksville, U.S. 64 passes through Lamar before ducking back under I-40 at Knoxville. It then rides the banks of Lake Dardanelle through London and across a levy right into Russellville, which is our next chapter.

POTTSVILLE TO MORRILTON

Potts Inn Tavern

On the other side of Russellville, you come to Pottsville, once home to one of the state's original taverns. Back before the Civil War, the U.S. government

Potts Inn Tavern at Pottsville. *Kat Robinson.*

worked out a couple of stagecoach routes to get mail from the East Coast to the West Coast. The southern of these two routes was created by John Butterfield and was called the Butterfield Overland. The stagecoaches that traveled this route carried both mail and passengers, and there were designated stops along this route. One of these stops is the old Potts Inn. Constructed in the 1850s by the family of Kirkbride Potts (a Pennsylvania man who married Pamelia Logan and had eleven children), it served as a tavern and waystop along the line. The Potts family lived in the house until the 1970s. Today, Potts Inn Tavern is a museum open to the public.

Bernell Austin: The Duchess Drive-In and the Fried Pickle

The next town along the way is Atkins, once known as the Pickle Capital of the World. In 1945, the Goldsmith Pickle Company located a plant in the town. Fifteen years later, a guy by the name of Bernell Austin leased a parcel of land from the Griffin Oil Company for ten dollars a month, set on building a drive-in. The little eatery called the Duchess Drive-In was pink and popular with plant employees who'd drop by after work.

Austin, known as "Fats" or "Fatman" to many of his constituents, looked for ways to increase business. In 1963, he struck on a new idea, battering and deep-frying hamburger dill slices and selling them for fifteen cents for a basket of fifteen. Thus the fried pickle was born.

Austin wasn't happy with that first recipe. He tweaked it and eventually settled on slicing dill pickles the long way and dropping them into a spicy batter before deep frying them to a golden brown. The recipe remains a family secret, though many claim that The Old South in Russellville has gotten ahold of the formula.

With the coming of the new interstate, Austin decided to line up and take advantage of the better traffic, building a new restaurant called the Loner Drive-In out toward the overpass and opening it in 1968. He closed the Duchess Drive-In in September of that year; two weeks later, an eighteen-wheeler ran into the building and destroyed it. Austin continued to operate the Loner Drive-In until he retired in 1978. He passed away in 1999.

Today, the recipe is definitively used at the Atkins Pickle Festival, held over two days every May. The family estimates some 2,500 orders are placed during the event each year.

Now, I would not claim to know Austin's famed recipe. But I do know the recipe that's been taught to me, and Stephanie Wilson has one of her own. If you're interested, check them out in the appendix.

Morrilton

Arkansas Tech University students know Exit 101 off Interstate 40 as "the Well." Blackwell is the first town across the border from Pope County into Conway County, and it's been home to two rival liquor stores for generations.

U.S. 64 dips south from there around Morrilton. The town has slowly migrated north to coalesce around the interstate, and the restaurants that once stood along the slow road are long gone. One of the first restaurants to catch on was the Morrilton Drive-Inn Restaurant in 1970. This is perhaps because of an ever-expanding menu that almost includes the kitchen sink; if they could figure out how to batter, deep fry and make edible that bit of plumbing, I have no doubt I'd see it on one of the many menu boards surrounding the ordering counter one day.

Pork chops, Frito pies, catfish, one-pound cheeseburgers, barbecue, meatloaf sandwiches, tacos, hamburger steaks, chicken-fried steaks, a full breakfast selection and ice cream and fried pies are just a sampling of the menu. Few restaurants survive on such a broad selection, but the Morrilton Drive-In thrives with it. Crowds of Razorback fans sometimes inundate the place; sometimes, tour groups stop in. Don't bother even trying to get in on a Friday night during football season—there won't be a place to sit unless you go right in the middle of the game, and then you'll be packed in with all the local fans once the game ends.

A block and a half away, you'll find YESTERDAY'S, Morrilton's longtime family get-together restaurant (I even got together with my folks there after graduating from Tech in May 1995). It's well known locally for steaks, burgers and an all-you-can-eat spaghetti and sausage night. It's been open since 1989.

Atkinson's Blue Diamond Café

On the west side of town, you'll find the Atkinson's Blue Diamond Cafe. There's been a restaurant there for about thirty years now, and it catches a

lot of the traffic from the Morrilton Packing Company, which makes Petit Jean Meats.

In 2004, two couples purchased the restaurant, renovated it and started it afresh. Earle and Pat Eichenberger and Garry and Karen Atkinson took on the task of creating a new menu for the place. Sure, putting everything together was a lot of work, but apparently the hardest thing to determine was the name. In the end, they decided to go with Blue Diamond, partly because of the Arkansas flag and partly because of Petit Jean Meat's Blue Label products.

The restaurant has become known for a great grilled chicken salad and a pile-up version of nachos that's topped with smoked chicken or beef. There's a signature sandwich called the Shaner with your choice of three meats, two cheeses and what bread you want and Bill's Dills, which are fried pickles battered when you order them. There's a little bit of everything, from pulled pork shoulder smoked in house to cheese dip and salsa, a daily plate-lunch special and plenty of Petit Jean Meats

products, such as hot dogs and the BLT. And they make what they call the Dandy Dog, battering their own Petit Jean hot dog for a local fair-style favorite. Add in that it's about the only place several counties around that does a mean Monte Cristo sandwich.

Of course, there are desserts, including about anything you could want to do with ice cream. Of note is the Hot Fudge Cobbler. Yes, you read that right. It's a bubbling-hot chocolate cobbler topped with whipped cream, ice cream and a cherry, and it's an absolute sin. But don't worry—they take out all the calories before it's served, so you're all right.

Atkinson's Blue Diamond Café in Morrilton. *Grav Weldon.*

The folks at Atkinson's Blue Diamond Café have been gracious enough to share the recipe for their homemade Dandy Dogs.

DANDY DOGS
ATKINSON'S BLUE DIAMOND CAFÉ, MORRILTON

2 (1-pound) packages Petit Jean hot dogs
Oil, for frying
4½ cups flour
3 cups cornmeal
2 tablespoons salt
2 tablespoons baking powder
6 tablespoons sugar
4 eggs
About 5 cups milk, or to desired consistency

Heat oil to 350 degrees. Blend all ingredients except hot dogs together. Insert wooden stick into hot dogs and dip one at a time into batter, completely covering each one. Fry until golden brown. Makes 16 Dandy Dogs.

Chapter 6

RUSSELLVILLE AND DARDANELLE
AT THE CROSSROADS

Two cities on either side of a lake and a bridge between. That's how the cities of Russellville and Dardanelle developed. The first of those permanent bridges was a pontoon bridge that spanned the Arkansas River, a scary two-lane wood-and-metal affair that was anchored in the river to "teepees" to keep it from bowing from the currents. It washed away three times during its lifespan. At the time, it was the longest pontoon bridge in the world.

In 1929, that bridge was replaced by a tall steel-truss model, which stood as a connection between the towns until 1971, when it was demolished to make way for the four-lane bridge that crosses the river today. The bridge takes Arkansas Scenic Highway 7 over the river, connecting the Ouachitas, the Ozarks and U.S. 64 with Arkansas Highway 22.

This was the crossing point, the place where travelers headed out of Fort Smith, crossed over to U.S. 64 on that suggested back route that shaved eighteen miles off the trip to Little Rock. And north of that crossing was the town of Russellville. Before its official name, the community was known as Chactas Prairie, the Prairie or Cactus Flats. Russellville's POM is the world's largest manufacturer of digital parking meters. It's the hometown of Jimmy Lile, the famous knife maker whose works appeared in the Rambo movies, and of Scott Bradley, who composed the music for the *Tom and Jerry* cartoons. It was the midpoint of construction on Interstate 40 between Little Rock and Van Buren during the 1960s. It's the home of Arkansas's only nuclear reactor, the Microplane grater kitchen tool, Arkansas Tech University and me—sort of.

Historic postcards show the world's longest pontoon bridge of its time at Dardanelle and the steel bridge that replaced it. *Arkansas Highway and Transportation Department.*

I'm a Little Rock girl. My folks are from a small town in southwest Arkansas called Gurdon, whose great claim to fame is the headquarters of the International Order of the Hoo Hoo (a lumber fraternity). I grew up in Little Rock, graduated from Parkview Arts Magnet High School in 1991 and returned here for good in 1999. But Russellville is also my home. I spent my four years of college exploring the logically laid-out street network, learning about life in a moderately sized town and generally falling in love with the idea that you can leave your car doors unlocked in the parking lot and that everyone at the local grocery store knows your name. I joke with people sometimes that one day I'll retire to 1993 Russellville. I'm only halfway kidding.

For a town of twenty thousand then (nearly thirty thousand today), Russellville has a lot of restaurants that continue to hang on.

THE OLD SOUTH

Time quells a lot of memories, but not all of them. I can quite clearly remember my first week in Russellville as a student at Arkansas Tech University. It was the first time I lived away from home. I learned a lot of things very quickly. I learned that at night, you could see stars from the center of campus, that there was little to no insulation on the outside of my room at Roush Hall, that driving up Mount Nebo with its little tight hairpin turns was a lot of fun and that you really only had two options for sitting down and eating overnight in town: the Waffle House or The Old South.

I wasn't the only student who quickly found out that the latter was the better choice. While you could only really hang out at the "Awful Waffle" as long as you had your plate in front of your face, at The Old South, you could sit up all night nursing a cup of coffee if you bought just one item off the menu. That item, in my case, was usually the fried honeybun—a Hostess honeybun removed from its package and heated in a skillet with a lump of margarine, dumped on a plate and presented with a fork. There were many nights I spent in the back room of the restaurant, usually in one of the round booths with one or more companions from school, poring over the notes for whatever test we were taking or, as became more common in my case, scribbling down yet another piece of poetry or prose for Mrs. Tyson's composition class or a slightly scandalous piece of fiction for B.C. Hall.

Historic postcard from The Old South in Fort Smith. *Historic Arkansas Museum.*

Those distant early 1990s days were packed from one end to another, and like with many college students, sleep just wasn't as important for me as it came to be later on. What most of us failed to grasp, though, was just how important the restaurant where we huddled happened to be to history.

See, The Old South was about forty-five years old about the time I was looking at twenty. In my late teens, I didn't really comprehend the value of the sleek art deco styling or of the time capsule that the place had become for the last remnants of the great Route 64, which, if not of the same cultural importance as Route 66, was certainly a byway of significance in the way this part of the country unfolded in the middle part of the twentieth century.

The restaurant was built in 1947, a couple years after the end of the Second World War. As much as today's residents of Russellville would like to believe that it's the one and only, it wasn't alone, and it wasn't the first—that was The Old South in Fort Smith, opened around 1945 at 711 Towson Avenue (now a parking lot for Sparks Regional Medical Center).

Here's what it all amounts to. The Old South wasn't a family start-up like other restaurants I've talked about. It was a concept restaurant—a franchise, at that—created as a turnkey operation. The original man with the plan was William E. Stell, an Oklahoma-born businessman who created and founded the National Glass and Manufacturing Company in Fort Smith back in 1929. The company created fixtures, furniture and metalwork for restaurants and department stores. It wasn't a far jump for Stell to develop a modular diner system to take advantage of the new automobile culture that was developing. Unlike the Streamliner design (which was a contained prefab unit), Stell's idea was for a modular, build-on-site system that could be adapted to the location. He employed the help of architect Glenn Pendergrass (he designed the El Chico restaurants around Dallas) to design the concept he envisioned.

The first, that Fort Smith store, was an experiment. Stell brought in a guy from New York City to form a menu—none other than Schwab's R.C. Strub. The approach of a Kansas City–style steakhouse menu was adapted for use in what would be a series of roadside diners. The idea was to create a restaurant quickly. And it did catch on.

No one knows for certain how many Old South restaurants were built, but the last "other" restaurant (in Camden, South Carolina) apparently closed in 2005. The original location was demolished in the 1970s. There were several in Oklahoma and Arkansas, most of which were given different names, such as the Little Rock location, which housed Gordon Adkins and the Ritz Grill.

The Russellville location, though, started quick and has endured for the ages. The last week of March 1947, Stell delivered on a contract to Woody Mays, owner of Woody's Classic Inn and Coffee Shop (the motel still operates today, though the coffee shop is long gone), and had the location built in just six days. It opened on April 4, 1947, on the outskirts of town.

Now remember, this was long before Interstate 40 ran coast to coast. While folks tend to recall Route 66 as the best way from Chicago to the California coastline, it wasn't the only way to get out there. Route 64 (which actually intersects with old Route 66 in Tulsa, Oklahoma) was the best way to get from the East Coast in North Carolina out as far as Arizona and took drivers on the most direct east–west route across Arkansas. Because of this, folks of all ilk traveled the highway, and when they came into Russellville, they stopped at The Old South for a bite. Didn't matter who they were, they stopped. That includes the likes of Ernest Tubb, B.B. King and even, yes, Elvis Presley.

Back in the 1990s, I didn't know what the place looked like inside during the day. I was too busy leading the extraordinarily packed life of a would-be band director and broadcaster, and the only time I managed to get inside was when I was pulling an all-nighter. Other Tech students made fun of the place, with rather crude names for the eatery. You might think it was the sort of place you wouldn't revisit later on, but it was. It didn't take me long after graduation and a whirlwind few months that sat me down in Jonesboro at my first TV job in 1995 for me to realize I missed the place.

It'd take me time to make a real return, and by that point, it was May 2008. I was pregnant and craving fried chicken, and it was, as always, crisply and heavily battered, greasy and served with that notorious salad on the side that wasn't much more than lettuce and carrot shreds—comfort food.

Since then I've dropped in from time to time, usually grabbing breakfast. And it's a breakfast I have always appreciated, pretty much from when I could afford something more than the fried honeybun. The corned beef from a can, the hash browns and eggs fried on a griddle top enhanced by well over sixty years of grease—enough to give you a heart attack if you ate it day after day—food for the soul when you were on the road and you didn't know for certain how long it would be before you got back home. Consider it a homecoming, if you will, a place to land for a lonely freelancer trying to get a scoop on a story to sell to whatever magazine would throw a little cash her way.

The Old South ceased being a twenty-four-hour operation sometime in that interim when I was growing up, living life and getting my head on straight. It couldn't compete with IHOP or the new Waffle House or the late-night coffeehouses with their posh lighting and even posher coffee menus. At The Old South, there's coffee, regular or decaf, and you can get cream and sugar if you want it, but that's about it. It's the sort of thing that apparently doesn't really appeal to today's college crowd (though I understand the hipsters really dig that sort of scene).

The place nearly ceased to exist altogether in April 2013, shut down for nonpayment of taxes. But folks around town have ties to the place, this old section of Americana, and they banded together and held a citywide yard sale and paid the taxes. And it's open again.

Sixty-six years is a pretty dang good run for any restaurant, even more so for a restaurant built in just six days. Whether The Old South survives this generation and the ones to come after it remains to be seen. But I think it's about time I plan to drop in and grab myself a bite. I might even order that damn fried honeybun again.

Brown's Catfish

If you want catfish and you're on the north side of the river, you head to Brown's Catfish. Started in 1980 as Brown's Country Inn by Al Brown as a full-service, mom and pop family restaurant, this place has kept the parking lot packed for well over thirty years.

Today, Al and his wife, Beth, operate the store with their grown kids. The catfish is, of course, the top draw, but there are other specialties, such as ribs served with what they call Charlie Casto's Famous BBQ Sauce, after the customer who allowed them to "borrow" the recipe a couple of decades ago.

Catfish 'N

I was a member of Tau Beta Signa, the band sorority (technically a fraternity—don't get me started) that paired with Kappa Kappa Psi and together were the organizations attached to Arkansas Tech University's Band of Distinction. For casual get-togethers, we'd gather at Mr. Burger. If it were a more upscale event, we headed across the river to Catfish 'N.

The relaxed location along the south bank of the Arkansas River was excellent for great views and post-dinner gatherings on the sandy shore for volleyball and sometimes even a bonfire. The old fish camp holds great memories for many of us.

Catfish 'N in Dardanelle. *Kat Robinson.*

The place opened in 1971 downstream from the dam. In 1980, Tim Tackett bought the place; he had been a dishwasher starting out there. He and his wife, Carole, have run it ever since, using Tim's grandmother's recipes for many things and sticking with a proprietary hush puppy recipe that folks ask for often. Today, it's a buffet that features catfish, boiled shrimp, fried chicken, lemon basil chicken breast, fried shrimp, hot vegetables, salads, biscuits and cobblers with ice cream.

It's worked for more than forty years, and not just for the community. Catfish 'N has been named in such publications as *USA Today, Gourmet, Newsweek* and *U.S. News and World Report*—pretty big praise for such an unpretentious place.

The Tacketts have been gracious enough to share one of their newer recipe adaptations for this book.

SWEET HOG WRAPPED CHICKEN
CATFISH 'N, DARDANELLE

4 boneless, skinless chicken breasts, cut into 1-inch cubes
1 pound sliced bacon, each slice cut into thirds
⅔ cup firmly packed brown sugar
2 tablespoons chili powder

Mix together brown sugar and chili powder. Roll chicken pieces in mixture. Wrap bacon around chicken and place on skewer. These may be grilled or baked.

To bake: place on baking rack coated with nonstick cooking spray. Bake at 350 degrees for 30 to 35 minutes.

To grill: Use medium heat. Turn every 5 to 7 minutes for even browning. Cook until chicken is thoroughly done.

Can be used as an appetizer or entrée. These may be prepared for cooking 24 hours ahead of time and kept in refrigerator.

This recipe adapted from Food Network.

EL TACO CASA

About a block west off Union Street (which goes over the Arkansas River Bridge), there's an old Mexican place still serving good Ark-Mex food. This is

El Taco Casa, which started up in 1978. It's not a big place or an expensive place, but the food is good and reasonable for any college student on a budget.

I say this because I was that college student on a budget back in 1993. So were some of the folks I hung out with, and one particular guy actually took me there for lunch as a date. Hey, at least the food was good.

OLD POST BAR-B-Q

Being an Arkansas resident who travels through the American South on occasion, I have consumed my share of barbecue. I've sampled dry rubs and wet ones, brisket and chicken, chopped meat and sliced meat. Before I developed my adult allergies, there were few things in this world that outclassed sloppy pork ribs in my book.

I've had sauces that have ranged from thin and vinegary to thick and spicy. I've dabbed on molasses doubling as sauce and savored Texas-style brisket without it. And everywhere I go, I tend to find a favorite barbecue palace to frequent.

But there's just one place in this world that makes a barbecue that tastes like what I think barbecue should taste like—to the very essence of the meat and the thickness of the sauce. That is Russellville's own Old Post Bar-B-Q.

I was introduced to this Arkansas Avenue eatery my first week of college while hanging out with fellow Tech band members. As with many of our get-togethers, dinner was a pick-up affair, with meat and bread and fixings for two hundred hungry musicians and flag line members. Though I'd grown up on the sweet vinegar tang of Sim's and the smoky, full-body taste of the Shack, there was something about this particular sauce that just shook me awake from my epicurean sleep. Between good smoky and juicy meat and a hearty, well-balanced sauce, I was happy and satisfied.

This eatery started up in 1979 on Old Post Road out on the south side of town—the road that goes out to the dam park and which used to be the overland route for the postal service—by Bob and Toni Munson. They moved it to its current location along Arkansas Avenue (Scenic Highway 7) in 1983. Today, it's run by Ray and Anna Black.

The restaurant changes little from year to year, though every couple years they shut down for a bit and do a thorough cleaning from top to bottom (maybe it's a Russellville thing; Whatta-Burger does it, too). Booths are private by nature, with high wood-beam backs that are surprisingly comfortable. There are tables, too, and lots of Coca-Cola memorabilia. In

Old Post Bar-B-Q in Russellville. *Grave Weldon.*

fact, unlike a lot of local restaurants, Old Post doesn't split its loyalties between the Razorbacks and Tech's own Wonderboys. During sports seasons, it's the Cyclones (Russellville High's team) that you'll see promoted here.

Old Post Bar-B-Q offers a lot of different choices, if you like meat. The menu sports an array of dinners: sliced beef, pulled pork, smoked ham and turkey, Polish sausage, chicken and ribs, available in a dinner or on a sandwich. There's a french dip and a nice variety of sides: beans, slaw, potato salad, fried okra, mac and cheese, "Kurley Q" fries and banana pudding. They offer a mean chef's salad with your choice of smoked meat, stuffed baked potatoes and chicken nuggets for the kids. Add in fried pickles and tater skins, and that's about all there is to the menu.

What's it really like, though? Well, my observations from one Tuesday evening in May 2008 were recorded on my blog. I had dropped in for an Old Post Special (a jumbo sandwich with choice of meat and two sides). As I wrote then:

> *You can hear the hum of conversation easily in the restaurant—a family of three talking about a dog the son was hoping his mom would let him keep, a couple of old men talking about high gas prices. From the back, the patter of gossip ranged from what was interesting on Dial-A-Trade that*

Chicken parmigiana at Mary Maestri's in Springdale. *Grav Weldon*.

Spaghetti and meatballs at The Venesian Inn in Tontitown. *Kat Robinson*.

The coconut meringue pie at Mama Z's in Tontitown. *Grav Weldon*.

The AQ Combo: fried chicken and spaghetti, found at the AQ Chicken House in Springdale. The "AQ" stands for Arkansas Quality. *Kat Robinson*.

Chicken dinner at the Monte Ne Inn Chicken Restaurant. *Grav Weldon*.

Cookies at Rick's Bakery in Fayetteville. *Grav Weldon*.

Left: The famed French-dipped sandwich at Ed Walker's Drive In in Fort Smith. *Kat Robinson*.

Below: The giant cheeseburger at Ed Walker's in Fort Smith. Note the normal-sized cheeseburger on top. *Grav Weldon*.

Opposite: Chocolate peanut butter cup, Chocolate Pile and Cherry Crisp pies at Miss Anna's on Towson in Fort Smith. *Grav Weldon*.

Left: Pancakes at Benson's Grill in Fort Smith. *Grav Weldon.*

Below: Pan-fried Boston Mountain quail at The Red Barn Steakhouse in Fort Smith. *Grav Weldon.*

Left: Grandma's Biscuits at The Red Barn Steakhouse in Fort Smith. *Grav Weldon*.

Middle: A sampling of dishes at Emmy's German Restaurant in Fort Smith. *Grav Weldon*.

Bottom: The Inferno Burger at Lewis' Family Restaurant in Fort Smith. *Grav Weldon*.

Top: The famous
Calico County
cinnamon rolls.
Grav Weldon.

Middle: The
Uncle Roman at
Steffey's Pizza
in Lavaca.
Grav Weldon.

Bottom: The big
doughnuts at
Craig's Family
Bakery in
Van Buren.
Grav Weldon.

The steak and three sauces at Kelt's Pub in Altus. *Kat Robinson*.

Harvested grapes at Post Familie Vineyards in Altus. *Grav Weldon*.

Top: Fried pickles.
Grav Weldon.

Bottom: Corned beef
hash and eggs with
hash browns, biscuits
and gravy at The Old
South in Russellville.
Kat Robinson.

Above: Smoked chicken at Old Post Bar-B-Q in Russellville. *Kat Robinson*.

Left: A Sissy burger and fries at Feltner's Whatta-Burger in Russellville. *Kat Robinson*.

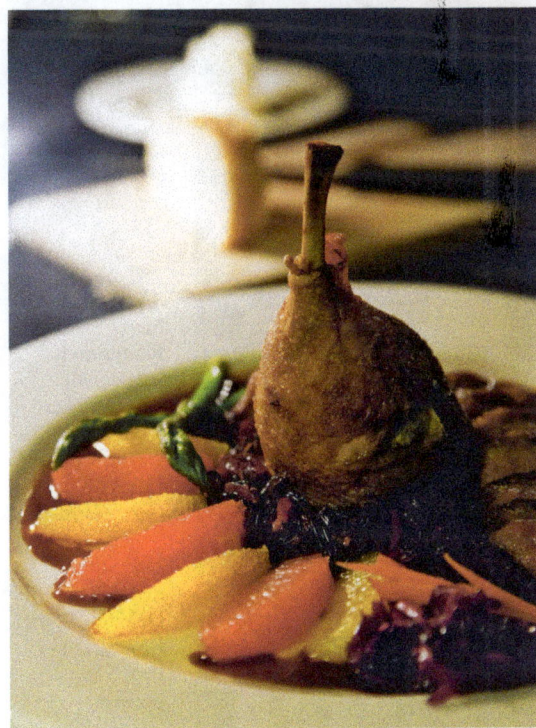

Opposite, top: Breakfast at Stoby's in Russellville. *Kat Robinson.*

Opposite, bottom: Oatmeal pie at Oark General Store. *Kat Robinson.*

Top: Trout Italiano at DeVito's Italian Restaurant in Eureka Springs. *Kat Robinson.*

Bottom: Classic preparation of half duckling at the Grand Taverne in Eureka Springs. *Grav Weldon.*

Above: Center Street Salsa Platter and homemade flour and corn chips at KJ's Caribe in Eureka Springs. *Grav Weldon.*

Left: Stuffed ravioli at DeVito's Italian Restaurant at Bear Creek Springs. *Grav Weldon.*

Left: A single cinnamon roll at Ferguson's Country Store and Restaurant in St. Joe. *Kat Robinson*.

Below: Chicken-fried chicken at the Chuck Wagon Restaurant in Bee Branch. *Kat Robinson*.

Top: The Barnburner at The Back Forty. *Kat Robinson.*

Middle: Fried catfish at the Pot o' Gold Restaurant near Heber Springs. *Kat Robinson.*

Bottom: The baked brie at the 178 Club in Bull Shoals. *Grav Weldon.*

day to what one of the younger girls was planning to do for her wedding. The sizzle of the deep fryer signaled the okra was in the grease, and soon, a young woman brought me a red tray with my lunch.

Like most places around these parts, you get fed—a lot. My beef sandwich took up an end of the oval platter, shared with a mess of fried okra and a cup of macaroni and cheese. The beef isn't the dry stuff of chain restaurants. Instead, the natural juices of the brisket are allowed to remain with the meat, making it juicy enough to eat without the sauce. But the sauce? Oh my. Can't go off without that sauce. It's the perfect balance between sweet and tangy, smoky and spicy.

The okra was nice and light—obviously just cooked, as evidenced by the heat. The mac and cheese was soft but not "gloopy" like you get at places where the sauce comes out of a can. Paired up with a cold iced tea, it was a lovely sight.

One oddity about Old Post is that it's one of the rare Arkansas barbecue establishments that treats coleslaw strictly as a side item, not a condiment. The barbecue sauce does tend to soak the bottom bun; for those taking theirs to go, I recommend inverting the sandwich top-down in the bag.

BIG RED DRIVE-IN

Travelers who take Interstate 40 tend to stop for a burger at either the old favorite (Feltner's Whatta-Burger) or the new upstart (CJ's Butcher Boy

Big Red Drive-In in Russellville. *Grav Weldon.*

Burgers, started in the former Waffle House in 2006). Locals know, though, that they can still get an old-time dairy-diner burger at Big Red Drive-In.

Keith and Anna Williams bought the place in 1971 after acquiring the Tastee Freeze on Fourth Street. Before then, the location was an A&W Restaurant. Today, Jo Ann Scott, Keith's daughter, is still running the place.

Inside the red and white concrete-block building, you'll find paneled walls and schoolroom chairs around tables. Order at the counter, take your number and have a seat. The Big Red burger is a half pound, the chicken-fried steak sandwich is a local favorite and there's fried chicken on the menu—and ice cream, too, of course.

FELTNER'S WHATTA-BURGER

In almost every city or town in America, there is one local hangout that's been around for ages and ages, the place you send out-of-towners to when you want to share a bit of your roots and culture.

In Russellville, hands down, it's Feltner's Whatta-Burger. There is no other place that comes close.

This isn't one of the chain—that would be Whataburger—and you won't find any orange Ws or cheesy promotions here. What you do find is good food in large portions at a restaurant splashed with the history of Russellville and Arkansas Tech University.

Bob Feltner built this landmark. The first Feltner's Whatta-Burger came off the grill in 1967. Whether it was an everything burger or plain or even a "Sissy" is lost to time.

The burgers are made on an assembly line that would make Henry Ford proud. When you walk in, a host or hostess is there in baseball cap and apron, waiting to take your order. Each order is written on a paper sack in that marvelous code that old man Feltner developed years ago. Your sandwich order is written on the top, followed by the side (french fries or onion rings) and the drink (sodas and fabulously thick milkshakes). Fried pies you ask for at the register.

After the server takes your order, that sack is handed back to the grill. The grill guys (and gals) look at the order, and it's called out. Meat gets flipped onto the grill and starts sizzlin'. When it's cooked, it's plopped onto buns and shuttled over via paper bag to the dressing area, where lettuce, tomato, pickles and condiments are all added to your custom order. The sandwiches

Bob Feltner. *Courtesy Missy Ellis.*

are wrapped, and hefty bags of fries or onion rings are dropped into the sacks with your sandwich. If you're eating in, they're placed on red trays instead.

Milkshakes are all hand dipped and measured, and whether it's something normal like chocolate or something exotic like peanut butter (my brother's favorite) or pineapple (mine), it's served up in a big Styrofoam cup.

That's the thing—old man Feltner never did like tiny quantities. He wanted you to be full when you left his restaurant. The fries come in two sizes, half orders and orders, and Tech students have been known to come across the street, order the full size and dine on them for a week.

There are all sorts of other things on the menu, too—like hot dogs and bologna sandwiches. You can even make your burger bigger by calling a Double (two patties of meat), a Double Double (that plus two pieces of cheese) and even a Triple (three patties). Until recently, the patties came fresh from John Garner Meats in Fort Smith, from a formula Bob Feltner thought up decades ago.

Most days, you can find a seat in one of the bright booths in the store. Locals will call in their orders and pick them up at the window, but if you've never been inside, you are missing something else. Each year before school starts, the restaurant is closed and cleaned from top to bottom. And that's when the décor is changed. Mr. Feltner used to change up the decor completely when he was still alive, but his daughter and her husband just change out a few things. They want it to still retain the feel it had all those years ago.

Some of it is corny—messages on wooden plaques with advice and folk sayings. There are pictures of three generations of Feltners, along with plaques won by local baseball teams and Wonderboy memorabilia. And you can't miss the awards from places like the *Arkansas Times* and magazines and such. There are letters from celebrities and politicians and plain folks like you and me. And there are the kites and stuffed animals that Mr. Feltner loved so much. Most of this stuff has been donated over the years, and all of it is about Arkansas. There's enough to complete a book right there.

And it's definitely a place of love. Mr. Feltner saved many a Tech student from lack of nourishment over the years. He'd run into kids and have a stack of business cards; when he heard a sad story, he'd scrawl out a note on the back of a card for a free meal or burger. Sometimes, he'd invite the kid to come over and work for a few extra dollars. To this day, a large part of the staff consists of Tech students trying to make it through college.

Mr. Feltner also helped me get my start. Back then, I was a young student with a yearning to be a radio star. One afternoon, I sat in that front booth with my single half order of fries, trying to figure out what I was going to do with my life and my potential career, and he came over and talked with me. I told him about my dreams, and my budding new show on the college radio station. He walked away and came back with a stack of his business cards with his familiar scrawl on the back. The way he figured it, he told me, if I gave people the chance to win a free Whatta-Burger meal every time I went on the air, more people would listen to me—and he was right.

Mr. Feltner died a few years ago, and his funeral was probably the biggest funeral anyone had ever seen in Russellville. People came from all over Arkansas and all around the United States to pay tribute to this man who gave so much. Sure, it might have only been a meal, but it was that sort of gesture of kindness that meant the world.

Today, Feltner's Whatta-Burger is run by his daughter and son-in-law, Missy and Randy Ellis. The place still stands across Arkansas Avenue from Arkansas Tech.

And in case you were wondering, a "Sissy" is just a way of preparing a Whatta-Burger, with just lettuce, tomato and mayo. Want it with a slice of American cheese? Ask for a Whatta-Cheese. And don't forget the fries.

TACO VILLA

Russellville has its own flavors, and one all the folks who have ever been able to be called local have experienced is the taco salad at Taco Villa. Started in 1974, the tiny brown restaurant on Fourth Street still offers the best deal on reasonably priced Mexican fare in town.

It's been nearly forty years since the place opened and twenty since I left Tech, but even today, you can still get that TV salad or the huge plate of nachos or the burrito—a two-handed full-of-everything burrito. The meat blend is still the same—not as spicy or salty as other fast-food taco places, but consistent—and it's always served with a heaping pile of shredded lettuce and that American-cheddar blend cheese.

The secret to the taco salad is that it is the exact same thing as the nachos, except upside down: the lettuce and tomatoes go on the bottom for the salad with the chips on the side, while the nachos are the chips, beef and cheese on the bottom with the tomatoes and lettuce all on the top. Taco Villa also does right by still melting real cheese on its nachos, rather than pouring it on.

Taco Villa on Fourth Street in Russellville. *Grav Weldon.*

OZARK MOUNTAIN SMOKEHOUSE

Back in 1946, Roy Sharp decided to smoke some meat. This was actually a pretty big thing.

See, as the story goes, Sharp was served smoked turkey at a party he attended way back in the 1930s. It was dry and salty, and as he told his wife later, he figured if he ever smoked his own meat he could do a better job than that.

It took about a decade, but eventually, Roy retired to the Ozarks and started smoking turkeys and hams in his barn. His friends would ask him to smoke one for them when he decided to fire it up. But Sharp burned the dang barn down.

That's how he came to build a smokehouse on the family land at Mount Kessler (now on the southwest side of Fayetteville). Thus Ozark Mountain Smokehouse was born. Over the decades, the business would expand to include nine shops in eight cities, and Roy's son Frank and his daughter-in-law Sara would continue the tradition.

In recent years, the business has pulled back, and now, just the manager-run stores keep up the tradition. There's Ozark Family Restaurant in Little Rock and the Ozark Mountain Smokehouse in Russellville. The Russellville location is poked into a lot off West Main catty-cornered from Kroger, and the folks there are still smoking their own meat. Open for more than thirty-five years, it's still the place to go for country-style breakfasts with slabs of smoked ham and for roast beef and roast turkey sandwiches piled high with smoked cheeses.

MADAME WU'S

These days, you can't swing a cat without hitting an Asian restaurant in Russellville. Chinese, Japanese and Thai are all available now. But the very first fine Asian dining experience to build a tradition in town was Madame Wu's. Since its opening in 1985, the Hunan hole in the wall on south Arkansas Avenue has hosted thousands at its linen-covered tables.

STOBY'S

During my college days, there were three in-town places to go for a fine dinner. You went to the I-40 Supper Club if you wanted an alcoholic beverage (which, being twenty-one when I graduated, wasn't an option to me most of my time there), you went to Cagle's Mill at the old Holiday Inn for a prime rib (today preserved by the same chef at the recently opened Opal Mae's downtown) or you celebrated with your friends at Stoby's.

Russellville's Stoby's is the second location for the business; the first is in Conway. I didn't actually darken the door of the original location for another decade, even after I'd become a regular at the short-lived third location in Jonesboro.

Stoby's is the creation of David Stobaugh. Back in 1977, he was about to graduate from the University of Arkansas in Fayetteville with a degree in banking and finance. One day, he was at a restaurant, and it occurred to him that running a restaurant was an honest way to make a living. So right out of college, he took a job as a grill cook at Western Sizzlin'.

He wasn't there long. A couple friends called him and asked if he'd run the new Danver's franchise coming into Conway, so he relocated that direction. He spent a short time there and then took on a variety of enterprises, including a bike-pedaled ice cream concession.

One day in 1980, out of work and broke, David walked into Mrs. Smith's Pie Shop on Donaghey and proposed a deal: he'd split the rent

Stoby's in Russellville. *Kat Robinson.*

with her if she'd let him go into business with her, making sandwiches to go along with her pies. What he didn't count on was the fact that Florence Smith was ready to be done with running a pie shop. She offered him the joint and then asked him to hire her, which he did. She worked for him for years to come.

Stoby's opened quietly. David had to sell his wife's car just to get enough money to buy food to sell. But it caught on, and business went so well that David opened the second location, in the old depot at Russellville, in 1984. He'd go on to open two other restaurants, and the cheese dip created at Stoby's would become ridiculously popular, first as a grocery store staple and then as the endorsed favorite of *American Idol* star Kris Allen.

About the time Kris Allen was getting ready to take the training wheels off his bicycle (that's supposition, of course—I have no idea if Kris Allen rides a bike, only that he's the age of my brother), I was learning what a great place Stoby's was. The cheese dip brought me in, like so many other local folks, but I was also charmed by a rail track overhead where a train would circulate. The Reuben wasn't bad, either.

Stoby's was the sort of place my mom would take me when she came up to visit me in Russellville. It was the place where I received my first recognition from any employer ever—from **KXRJ** Radio, sure, but I'd never had a plaque to put on the wall to tell people I did a good job at radio before. When I moved out of the dorm in 1993, when I was scraping by sharing rent with four roommates and working as a pizza delivery girl in between classes, I'd celebrate a good week of tips with a Saturday morning breakfast of corned beef hash and eggs. And about the time I really started to feel homesick three years later in my little apartment in Jonesboro, there was a Stoby's that appeared four blocks away like providence had placed it there.

The heart of Stoby's isn't the cheese dip; it's the Stoby, a sandwich made with three meats and two cheeses with a choice of condiments and vegetation on your choice of bread. The choices include ham, smoked turkey or Petit Jean smoked sausage, salami or bologna; American, Swiss, cheddar, mozzarella, provolone, pepper Jack or Monterey Jack cheeses; lettuce and tomato, mayo or mustard; pita, bun, whole wheat, sourdough or rye. It's a sandwich to build a restaurant on.

For a brief time, David's wife, Patti, operated PattiCakes Bakery in the building to the west of the depot, before moving it behind the Conway location. But always the restaurant keeps going, with generations of proud parents taking their Arkansas Tech students out for a meal on game day or after graduation, and a satisfied community darkening the doors on a regular basis.

BUTTERMILK BISCUITS
STOBY'S, CONWAY/RUSSELLVILLE

5 pounds all-purpose flour
2 cups sugar
1 tablespoon salt
1 tablespoon baking powder
2 cups lard
½ gallon buttermilk

Preheat oven to 350 degrees.

Sift together all dry ingredients. Cut in lard with clean fingers until mixture is consistency of coarse sand. Add buttermilk until all the liquid is incorporated.

Working quickly, place dough on lightly floured table and roll out with a floured pin.

Using an official Stoby's Biscuit Cutter*, dip cutter in flour for each biscuit. Press down in one motion, being careful not to twist. Cut out one biscuit at a time and push dough together after each cut.

Place each biscuit on a sheet pan lined with parchment paper. Bake at 350 degrees for 30 to 35 minutes or until golden brown.

*An official "Stoby's Biscuit Cutter" is a large glass with the bottom punched out. Twisting the cutter can pinch the dough and cause the biscuit to not rise properly.

Chapter 7

SCENIC HIGHWAY 7 AND THE BUFFALO RIVER HIGHLANDS

Arkansas Highway 7 received its designation in 1926, when the Highway Department worked through our rather eclectic road-naming system and fixed things to align better with our neighboring states. In the 1930s, the wives of the Rotary Club folks in the area worked to get a scenic spot carved out alongside the road halfway between Russellville and Harrison. The spot, now called Rotary Ann, stands as a good spot to get out, stretch your legs and take a look around.

And what a view: the middle section of the Ozarks spans roughly from the Pig Trail (Highway 23) on the west to close to U.S. 65 in the east. Bisecting it neatly is the Buffalo National River—the nation's first national river, designated thusly in 1972 after marvelous work by U.S. congressman John Paul Hammerschmidt.

Highway 7 once went border to border; its terminus at Diamond City close to the Missouri border only comes now because of Bull Shoals Lake. It's the longest Arkansas state highway.

The completion of Interstate 40 across Arkansas in 1973 only hastened people to visit the northern stretch of the road; the opening of Dogpatch USA in 1968 really started it. Attractions all along its length popped up, from Mystic Caverns to Booger Hollow ("population 7, counten one coon dog"). There were motor courts, flea markets, craft stores and, yes, restaurants. Heck, there were cafés and diners and drive-ins all over the Ozarks.

Dogpatch USA closed down in 1994, and though Highway 7 had become the first designated Scenic Byway in Arkansas the year before, its businesses dried up. Much of the same happened throughout the Ozarks, as rural folk left the farms and hollows for metropolitan life.

But today, there's a new boom of tourists, from those who want to hop on a motorcycle and explore the curves and bends of the road to the elk watchers headed to Boxley Valley and canoeists, kayakers and hikers who want to experience the Buffalo National River. And there are restaurants that hang on throughout the rural Ozarks to this day.

OARK GENERAL STORE

The Oark General Store is, as far as anyone knows, the oldest and longest continuously operating general store in the state of Arkansas. But that doesn't make it the oldest continuously operating restaurant in the state. I've had folks tell me this, but now that I have the scoop, I want to set the record straight.

You may remember my hearty recommendation for pie at the store in *Arkansas Pie*. What we didn't talk about there was the state of affairs the place has been in of late or where the pie comes from. It's tricky.

See, the little general store was opened up back in 1890, a hub for a community cut off from a good portion of the rest of the world. Its location, not far from the Mulberry River atop a plateau in the Ozark National Forest, meant it was very isolated, and even today, there's no cellphone signal anywhere near town.

It did, however, have the corner on the market in the tiny little burg. Residents came down to the store any time of year to pick up seeds, sundries and groceries and for some good-natured gabbing, too. In the summer, the local kids came by to spend a nickel on candy; in the winter, the old men of the area huddled up around a potbellied stove in the middle of the place and told stories of warmer times.

Over those many years, it was likely as not that someone was cooking. From the store's inception, there was always some sort of ready-to-eat food there. Sometimes, there was an old woman who was a cook, and sometimes, there wasn't. There were wedges of cheese, pickled eggs and jerky by the register.

Sometimes, a single family owned the place, and sometimes, they didn't. See, the Oark General Store has changed hands multiple times over the years. But because it's in such an isolated place, it's needed to stay open, so it's never closed down. The community has seen to that.

The current owners, though, aren't what you'd expect. In 2012, Brian and Reagan Eisele came to Oark to stay. The couple's story began not in Arkansas—or in Washington, D.C., where both of them worked—but in the

Inside the Oark General Store. *Grav Weldon.*

breakaway former Soviet republic of Azerbaijan. Reagan Highfill worked for then congressman John Boozman of Rogers. Brian Eisele worked for Congressman Joe Wilson of South Carolina. The two were part of a staff group touring oil fields and learning about the latest emerging ideas in the energy industry overseas when they met and fell in love in February 2010.

Reagan is from around here—Hartman, to be exact—and she graduated from Tech in 2006. Brian graduated from the University of South Carolina in 2005. They came back here in April 2012 to marry at Boxley Valley. While down here preparing for the wedding, Reagan saw a notice in the newspaper announcing the Oark General Store was for sale. She mentioned it to Brian, and three weeks after they took the matrimonial plunge, they took another one—into store ownership

It has not been easy, but it has been interesting. And they happened to step in at a time when the restaurant has been gaining popularity on several fronts. It's a fuel and food stop for campers heading further back into the Ozark wilds, a chance to prepare for a Mulberry River float, a mid-drive lunch stop for motorcyclists and a destination for food lovers looking for pie.

The Eiseles have experienced a lot of unusual events. They were pretty much unprepared for their first experience of Bikes, Blues and BBQ, a five-day festival that brings an estimated 400,000 motorcycle enthusiasts to Fayetteville and the rest of northwest Arkansas. They reportedly went through five hundred burgers in a single day during that event. They've hired back some of the employees who worked under former management at the store. They've brought in satellite TV and created a Wi-Fi hotspot, the only one within a twenty-mile radius and a blessing in an area where cellphone service is nonexistent. And they've learned how to make pie—no, really, before taking on the store, neither Brian nor Reagan had any substantial restaurant experience, and they're learning as they go along.

They've learned well, though. On my most recent visit, I stopped in for a burger and onion rings. I asked if the onion rings were homemade and was asked if I'd like them to be. When I responded in the affirmative, the cook got about making onion rings from scratch. And talking with Brian before I hit the road, I was suckered into a slice of pie (not that I needed much convincing), a slice of oatmeal pie I ended up consuming while talking with him about how the place was shaping up.

It's all come together. The fantastic burgers from past incarnations are still there, great pies of half a dozen varieties are always in the case and there's always a conversation going on within the walls, just like with those gentlemen of old who came to warm themselves around the stove with gossip and coffee.

The Eiseles have been good enough to share one of their recipes with me especially for this book.

CAT-HEAD BISCUITS AND GRAVY
OARK GENERAL STORE, OARK

Biscuits:
4 tablespoons shortening
2 cups WR self-rising flour
Buttermilk
1 stick butter, softened

Rib-Sticking Bacon Gravy:
1 to 1½ cups bacon grease
1 cup all purpose flour
1 tablespoon salt
1 tablespoon pepper
½ to 1 gallon whole milk

Preheat oven to between 400 and 425 degrees.

In mixing bowl, cut shortening into flour. Add buttermilk and mix thoroughly until dough reaches desired consistency. If dough is too sticky to work, add more flour, a little at a time. If dough is too dry, add buttermilk until consistency is correct.

Grease a baking pan and then lightly coat the top of dough with flour—this will help keep your hands from sticking to the dough. Use your hands to softly compact the flour into dough. With a utensil roughly the size of a standard wooden spoon, scoop out a ball of dough and work gently with your hands to smooth it out. Place balls of dough onto greased pan until dough is gone.

With a pastry brush or paintbrush, spread softened butter on tops of biscuits. Then, place the baking sheet in preheated oven for about 25 to 35 minutes, or until golden brown on top. Halfway through baking, repeat spreading butter on tops of biscuits.

When biscuits are desired color and size, take out of oven and spread butter over tops one more time. The biscuits should soak in the butter at this point.

In an iron skillet, heat bacon grease to medium-high on stovetop. Mix in salt and pepper with grease. When grease gets hot enough to make the flour sizzle, add in all-purpose flour while stirring constantly, eliminating clumps. Roux needs to reach a creamy consistency. If roux is too runny, add more flour a little at a time. If roux is too dry, add more bacon grease in same fashion. It's important to keep an eye on the flour, as it browns quickly. Use your nose to determine when the browning starts (we think it smells like popcorn), and mix in your milk once the flour is good and browned. Remember to stir constantly. Turn heat down to a high simmer and reduce your gravy to desired consistency. You can always add more milk later to thin the gravy, if needed.

The Eiseles say: "Two of our favorite ways to enjoy: 1) Split biscuit into two halves and pour gravy on both sides. 2) Crumble biscuit, add crumbled bacon and pour gravy on top. Avoid trips to doctor or cholesterol checks for a few days."

WAR EAGLE MILL

The drive up to War Eagle is not one you take quickly. No matter where you come from, you end up on windy, scenic, two-lane roads with miles of sky and fields aplenty.

Approaching from the south, you round a bend, and suddenly, you're glancing out over a verdant plain below, green dotted with the red of farm buildings and the far-off sight of a three-story structure. That is your destination.

You snake down the side of the hill, roll out into a field and wonder at the sign that states, "War Eagle Craft Mill, next 10 exits." Exits? You're in a cow field, for heaven's sake! Roll right with the road, down past a couple barn-type buildings on the right and a couple houses on the left, and then, you're at the bridge.

The bridge at War Eagle is nothing to sneeze at. It's a 1907 original, an old wood- and steel-framed century-old monument to time, arching its single lane out over the greenish river just down from the water break and coming to a landing beside the big red building you saw a mile back from on high. You have to slow down, to make sure no one's coming from the other side, before you ease on over and back onto the security of the gravel. You have arrived at War Eagle Mill.

The big gravel lot to the right is usually dotted with cars and motorcycles, sometimes with people just getting out of their vehicles, stretching their legs and visiting the facilities on the far side of the lot. Sometimes, there will be children there with handfuls of corn from the converted candy machine, toddling after the ducks and geese that tend to wander up from the river below. Sometimes, there's just the hum of the afternoon and the swish of the waterwheel.

Up the stairs and past the "No Wet Feet" sign, you enter the mill and are greeted with the ever-present churning and grinding of the millstone and machinery. Sometimes, one of the folks working back in the rear will pour in whole grains to be busted apart by the stones. Or there will be a couple people asking questions about the mill's operation. It always smells good.

Shoppers come and go, checking out the calico and paper bags of flour, cornmeal and grains or sampling some of the dips and jellies that are thoughtfully shared. There are jams, salsas, cookies and all sorts of mixes, as well as oven mitts and trivets and even fresh-baked bread in tiny loaves to snack on, if you're hankering for something to take with you. And there's that smell—not just of the grains but of something else, something from the oven—that draws you upward.

You climb the stairs to the second floor, where all manners of cookware and quilts await. This is where you can find your nonedible souvenirs of the day, the

War Eagle Mill and the War Eagle Bridge. *Kat Robinson.*

knives and stones and the honkin'-big cast-iron Dutch ovens. And you can look down from a number of windows on the water, waterwheel and bridge below.

But the scent drives you further upward, and you find yourself in the Bean Palace, the third floor of the mill, with a hard-to-deny menu of simple things, such as beans and cornbread, a cornbread sandwich or, heaven help us, cobbler. Bits of history are tacked on angled ceilings and walls, bits of a past that's embraced and treasured by those who work here and those who choose to make the trek, over and over again, to visit Arkansas's only working gristmill of its kind.

For generations, the power of the War Eagle River has been harnessed to mill grain for the Ozarks. Farmers would bring bags and bushels of corn and wheat from their fields to the mill to have the grain ground for their bread and sustenance. The mill's history spans back to 1832, when the first mill and dam were built by Sylvanus and Catherine Blackburn. Everything washed away in a flood in 1848. The second, built on the foundation of the first, became the heart of a community with an attached sawmill and a blacksmith shop, church and school all on the same property. It was destroyed by Confederate troops, burned to the ground three days before the Battle of Pea Ridge in 1862.

Sylvanus's son James built the third mill in 1873, but instead of using water power as his father had in the previous two mills, he used a steam-powered turbine to operate the machinery. It burned in 1924, and the foundation sat barren for nearly fifty years.

A man name Jewell Medlin and his wife, Leta Mae, purchased a cabin on top of a hill that included the mill foundation in the deed. Jewell contacted his daughter Zoe and asked if she would be interested in running a gristmill. They successfully reopened the War Eagle Mill on the same foundation in 1973, one hundred years after the opening of the third mill.

This fourth mill is powered by an undershot wheel, the only such device operating in all of Arkansas. Zoe and the man who would become her husband, Charlie Caywood, ran the mill for thirty years. They sold it in 2004 to Marty and Elise Roenigk of Eureka Springs, the owners of the Crescent and Basin Park Hotels. Today, Elise is the sole owner, Marty having been the victim of a car accident in June 2009.

The wheel goes whenever it goes—all the time. That's the nature of running water. The mill is open every day during most of the year, and every weekend through the dormant months (January and February).

Then there are the fairs. Every May and October, these massive events take over the landscape and bring thousands to the area, ninety thousand attendees in the spring and over a quarter million in the fall. For a few days each year, War Eagle becomes the biggest town in Arkansas (yes, even bigger than Little Rock) with vendors, live entertainment and arts and crafts at the War Eagle Craft Fair. It's hard to imagine—looking out from the window on the third floor of the mill and savoring a cornbread sandwich—the pastoral landscape beyond the river, green and quiet.

War Eagle Mill Bridge. *From historic postcard.*

War Eagle Mill isn't just a quiet three-story gristmill any more. It's big business, with a website drawing in folks to order products and a bustling retail business with flours and meals placed in stores all over Arkansas and the surrounding states.

Still, most of the sales come from folks who make the pilgrimage from Rogers or Harrison or Eureka Springs and load up on the bags of flours and jars of jam and preserves. There's been some small controversy with fans over the recent move to paper bags from the traditional cloth sacks replaced at the beginning of 2013, but the reasoning comes from the fact that most folks aren't making garments out of flour sacks any more.

The business continues, despite years that sometimes bring flood or snow. The eatery atop the mill also does well. The Bean Palace is certified USDA organic. Besides the sodas available by can, just about everything there could qualify. Bread, cornbread and pastries are all made from the grains ground downstairs; beans, smoked meats and fresh vegetables make up much of the rest of the menu. In the morning, there are pancakes and waffles and French toast served with smoked meats and eggs; at lunch, there are cornbread sandwiches, stews, soups and salads. And there's always a cobbler, hot and ready, and Mason jars of tea, all swaddled in that fantastic air of history.

CORNMEAL PANCAKES
WAR EAGLE MILL, ROGERS

1 cup WEM yellow cornmeal
½ cup WEM white whole wheat or
    WEM all-purpose flour
1½ teaspoons baking powder
1 tablespoon sugar
½ teaspoon salt
1¼ cups milk
1 egg
1 tablespoon vegetable oil or melted butter

In a medium size bowl, sift dry ingredients. Add milk, egg and oil to dry ingredients and mix until just blended.

Oil and heat griddle to medium low. Drop batter by tablespoonfuls onto griddle. Flip when surface is covered with bubbles and cook another 1 to 2 minutes on second side.

THE BEAN PALACE BLACKBERRY COBBLER
THE BEAN PALACE AT WAR EAGLE MILL

Filling:
10 cups fresh blackberries or mixed berries, or 2
    (16-ounce) packages frozen berries
1¼ cups sugar
6 tablespoons WEM all-purpose flour
¼ teaspoon salt

Crust:
3 cups WEM all-purpose flour
½ teaspoon salt
¾ cup butter or shortening
½ cup ice water

Blackberry cobbler at the Bean Palace. *Kat Robinson.*

In a large bowl, stir together berries, sugar, flour and salt. Set aside.
Preheat oven to 375 degrees.

In large bowl, combine flour and salt. Then, cut butter into flour mixture with a pastry cutter or in food processor. Stir or pulse (about six pulses) ice water into flour. Form into a soft ball. Divide dough into two pieces.

Turn out on floured surface and pat or roll one piece into a rectangle to fit the bottom of an 11 x 13 baking pan. Pour berries into pan over crust.

Roll second ball into rectangle that touches edges of pan when placed on top of berries. Press edges of crust onto pan.

Prick top crust with a fork. Bake 55 minutes.

CLIFF HOUSE INN

Over on Scenic Highway 7 stands a spot where you can get a beautiful view of what's referred to as the Arkansas Grand Canyon while having coffee and breakfast—the Cliff House Inn.

Opened in 1967, it's the home of a ubiquitous pie developed by Francis McDaniel, one of the many owners. Francis wanted a special biscuit and a signature pie for the place. She developed a meringue-crusted, sweet cream and pineapple-filled wonder called the Company's Comin' Pie, which was named the official state pie of the Arkansas Sesquicentennial in 1986.

Today, the inn is owned by Bob and Becky McLaurin. It's one of those rare places where you can still have sugar-cured ham for breakfast and where you can peruse a souvenir shop after you dine. When you go, budget extra time to sit out on the deck and take in the view of the beautiful Ozark hillsides carved by the Buffalo National River, which spread out for miles and miles.

The Cliff House Inn folks have graciously allowed me to share these recipes.

Cliff House Inn near Jasper. *Grav Weldon.*

150

SUGAR-FREE APPLE PIE
CLIFF HOUSE INN, JASPER

5 or 6 Granny Smith apples, sliced
7¼ teaspoons Equal artificial sweetener
1 teaspoon cinnamon
¼ teaspoon nutmeg
3 tablespoons cornstarch
Store-bought or homemade pie crusts

Preheat oven to 350 degrees.
   Blend all ingredients well. Pour mixture into unbaked pie crust. Place top crust over the apples and pinch around the edges. Brush with butter and cut slits into top. Bake for one hour.

COMPANY'S COMIN' PIE
CLIFF HOUSE INN, JASPER

6 egg whites
1 teaspoon cream of tartar
2 cups sugar
1 teaspoon vanilla
1 sleeve saltine crackers, crushed
½ cup chopped pecans

Topping:
1 small container whipped topping
3 tablespoons sugar
2 tablespoons crushed pineapple

Beat egg whites until fluffy. Add cream of tartar and sugar. Beat 25 minutes or until stiff.
   Stir in vanilla. Stir in crackers and pecans by hand.
   Spray two pie pans with nonstick spray. Divide mixture evenly between pans. Spread mixture in pan, forming a crust. Bake at 285 degrees for 25 minutes or until done.
   Combine topping ingredients. Pour into pie shell. Serve and enjoy.

Rita's

Along Arkansas Highway 27 in the tiny town of Hector, there's this little place that just keeps on going. Rita's Restaurant started up in 1993 to feed a community, which it still does, every single day of the week.

It's either your jumpin'-off point or your return point for when you'd like to dash off through one of the most remote sections of the Ozark Mountains. Highway 27 kicks and bucks its way through the countryside, finally coming up to be tamed at the town of Marshall fifty-four miles away. That mileage will take you an hour and a half, easy, and yes, you'll do it in that time, unless you don't value your life much.

When you do return and grab a bite at Rita's after a day behind white knuckles on the steering wheel or handlebars, you'll do yourself good to order the smothered steak over rice. A fortifying meal is necessary after such a strenuous journey. And if you're smart, or if the day has eaten away at your resources, you'll want to get a slice of whatever pie is offered.

Top Rock Drive-In

The first thing to note about the Leopard Burger is that it isn't actually made of leopards. Nor is it spotty. In fact, the only reason behind the name of the enormous burger offered at Top Rock Drive-In up in Alpena (open since 1978) is that it is the name of the school mascot. Still, there is a bit of relief to be found in the fact that no cats were harmed in the creation of this burger.

It's a big, fat burger—both tall and wide. It's a single hand-formed, griddle-smashed patty, charred all over its edge, every crack filled with American cheese (melted directly onto it) and perched on top of thick slices of tomato, a green leaf of lettuce, hamburger dills, fresh, chopped onion and a bun fried open-side down in a buttered pan. The buns come from the Mennonite bakery in Harrison.

The Leopard Burger at Top Rock Drive-In. *Kat Robinson.*

Loree's Cattleman's Restaurant

The drive to Eureka Springs from Harrison across U.S. 62 has always been interesting, with honey and apple stands, craftsmen, cabins and the occasional restaurant dotting the countryside.

In the Green Forest community, the next decent-sized town west of Alpena, you'll find Loree's Cattleman's Restaurant. You can't miss it because it's at the highway end of the North Arkansas Sale Barn. That's no joke. Open since 1958, the restaurant serves hot food to the community and the cowboys who come through. Wednesday is sale day, and yes, you can hear the auctioneers calling cattle for the block while you fill your plate from the buffet. On Friday and Saturday nights, you come to hear the owner's show.

Loree Pound Blackburn was born into a show family of ten children who were all raised in Texas. Her father, Tom Pound, was a voice and music teacher who took her, three of her sisters and her mom out traveling the country, performing shows and doing evangelistic work as the "Six Pounds of Music." They eventually settled in Eureka Springs, where they had a show for years. After Tom died, Mama Jane and the sisters continued to perform. And now Loree has Cattleman's Restaurant.

The place is a crossroads for ranchers, cattlemen and locals looking for a good bite to eat. Breakfasts are massive, the burger is a third of a pound and there's hot beef on the dinner menu—but no traditional steak, just a fantastically good chicken-fried steak.

GARNER'S DRIVE-IN

Berryville is the last community before you head into Eureka Springs when you're westbound on U.S. 62. While its more famous neighbor lacks even a stoplight in town, Berryville is a comparative metropolis, with chain restaurant outlets and a Walmart Supercenter.

But there's still a little drive-in serving up good burgers and shakes. That's Garner's Drive-In. Back in the early 1970s, Charlie Garner was looking for something to do in his later years. He and his wife, Frances, purchased the tiny little building about a block off the square and started up Garner's Drive-In. The original sign still stands out front; it appears to have once been a Dari De Lite

Charlie passed away in 1992, nearly fifty years after he'd married Frances. She continued with the business for a few more years before handing over the business to her daughter. Frances died in 2012, but Charlene Elkins and future generations of the family will keep the drive-in going.

Chapter 8

EUREKA SPRINGS

Motor Courts and Melting Pot

How do you get to Niagara Falls from Arkansas? Just follow U.S. 62. The wandering road will take you on a diagonal journey across the nation—all the way to Carlsbad Caverns and even El Paso—and in Arkansas, it slides across the northernmost part of the state, providing amazing views and a path through motor court history.

But what do motor courts have to do with restaurants? The little cafés at the heart of many of these little motor camps became the first, and sometimes only, impression for folks heading from one place to the next. And in the case of Eureka Springs, those folks were coming to town for health, relaxation and a good time.

U.S. 62 provided the perfect highway to come to Eureka Springs. Often called the Ozark Highland Trail, Ozark Trail or even the Ozark Skyway, the highway enters the state not far from Prairie Grove Battlefield State Park (a crucial Arkansas battle site during the Civil War), rolls up to Fayetteville and darts north concurrently with I-49 and U.S. 71. It slides off at Rogers and continues up past Garfield and Pea Ridge National Battlefield (another important Civil War site) and Gateway (past Martin Greer's Candies), cutting around and through the mountains to the twists of Eureka Springs. On the other side, the mountains ease a bit and U.S. 62 slides eastward through Berryville, Green Forest and Alpena, picking up U.S. 412 before joining up with U.S. 65 through Harrison. (We'll talk about where U.S. 62 goes later in the book.)

Before there was a Route 62, the road that went through Arkansas was known as the Ozark Trail, and it was, for people in that part of the country, the major way to get across north Arkansas or south Missouri before Route 66. The Ozark Trails Association, which was created to promote good roads, create usable maps and set highway markers, was created in 1913 by William Hope Harvey, also known as William "Coin" Harvey, whose most famous undertaking was Monte Ne. (Go back to page 36 to learn a bit more about Harvey.)

To put all that into perspective, Henry Ford's Model T was first manufactured and released in 1908. The idea of paved roads taking on the way they did in less than five years was just a hint of what was to come as America shifted from trains in the nineteenth century to automobiles in the twentieth.

Without paved roads, those cars weren't going anywhere, especially in the Arkansas Ozarks, where the stretch around the upper portions of the White River stands crooked and steep thanks to the river's millennia of cutting through the plateau. Dirt and gravel just wash away. Now, Eureka Springs had already been established as a place to take in the spring waters, with their healing properties (there are sixty-three springs throughout the city), and the folks who came there mostly did so by train, so the railroad did have its pull. But—and you'll come to know this about the place if you spend any time with the folks who call Eureka Springs home—the powers that be quickly saw the need to capture those folks who traveled by car and keep them coming back.

See, around 1910, there were more modern medical practices coming into vogue, and the idea of healing springs was being disavowed by the medical community. Without that traffic, who was going to make the trek to Eureka Springs and why? Was it worth it to pay for a journey by train or struggle to get through in a car or by horse?

So in comes Claude A. Fuller. He served as mayor of Eureka Springs over two different spans—once from 1906 to 1910 and then from 1920 to 1928. In the time between his terms, Fuller was a prosecuting attorney for several adjoining counties. During that time, he supported Charles H. Brough, the twenty-fifth governor of Arkansas. One of Brough's biggest contributions to the state was the establishment of a camp for convicts—whose labor was used to build a road from the town to Seligman, Missouri—near Eureka Springs.

Fuller was a pretty smart guy. When he was reelected in 1920 to the mayorship, he knew about the new state law that meant the state would pay half the cost of paving highways through towns if the town would pay the other half. He arranged for that convict labor to be used in cutting and paving roads through the limestone ridges around and through Eureka Springs on a winding path that took the road right through the middle of everything.

More than that, Fuller managed to get himself elected to Congress, where he was instrumental in getting the fledgling U.S. 62 routed along this new paved path. Voila, Eureka Springs was on one of the first paved stretches through the Ozarks.

Along those stretches that weren't already taken up with homes, spas and the like, motor camps sprang up. These were places where motorists coming to town could pull up, set up a tent or sleep in their vehicle and have a place to stay while they were enjoying the town. Sure, there were boardinghouses and inns and the like, but your average joe might not have the funds to cover a stay in a roofed building after that trek.

The camps were common, and they often included a café or tavern of some sort because those folks have to eat. And over the years, those motor camps would be replaced with motor courts, the single-story lodging for folks traveling by car where they could have the benefit of a roof over their heads, a bed to sleep in and a bath of their own. Eureka Springs had several camps and then dozens of motor courts, and today, you'll find everything from motor courts (or motels) to hotels, fine bed-and-breakfasts, cabins and cottages. And there are all sorts of restaurants, almost all of them locally owned and created (the town's chain outlets are limited to single stores for McDonald's, Pizza Hut and Subway)—some seventy unique eateries that serve not only a town with a permanent population of just over two thousand but also a consistently booming tourist influx that drives nearly three quarters of a million tourists to the town each year.

One of those eateries traces its lineage all the way back to the 1920s, to one of those original motor camps along Route 62.

To learn more about Eureka Springs and its unique history, including how Mayor Fuller got the highway through, check out *Hidden History of Eureka Springs* by Joyce Zeller.

MYRTIE MAE'S

On one of the westernmost ridges in the town lay a campground first opened in the 1910s. The Tower Heights Park Campground, established in 1914 by Sam Leath, had places to pitch your tent around a large concrete-

Camp Leath. *From historic postcard.*

floored pavilion that had, among its amenities, kitchen equipment, including refrigerators. We're talking top of the line here. It only cost a quarter to stay the night.

Before the end of the 1920s, Leath had converted his property into Camp Leath, believed to be Eureka Springs's first motor court. From the west, motorists would enter under an archway, "check in" with the management and claim a cabin for the night or week. The little log cabins weren't much—tiny one-room affairs with barely enough room for a bed—but sleeping in a bed under a roof sure beat sleeping on the ground under the stars.

There was a woman who lived in a house right next door who vested a stake in Camp Leath. Her name was Myrtie Mae Barrett. Myrtie Mae was a widow with six mouths to feed, and she was smart as a whip. She'd spent her years in a variety of careers—farm wife, practical nurse and cook—and she saw an opportunity. After trying out the idea with a couple of test runs, she opened her own dining room to strangers, advertising with a board nailed to a tree near the camp's entrance the kitchen's offering of "Home-Style Chicken Dinners." To the travelers who came to stay at the camp, if dinner meant the choice between warming up pork and beans in a can over a rudimentary stove or sitting down at a kind woman's table and eating fried chicken, it wasn't a hard choice to make.

Myrtie Mae was a strong woman, that's for sure. She served the same thing for lunch and dinner each day: fried chicken, vegetables (usually whatever was in season), mashed potatoes, rich cream gravy, homemade jams and jellies and hot homemade bread with fresh-churned butter, all served family style at her table. She learned how to make things happen quickly. She could open the door, count the travelers, invite them in and take off through the house to the back, where she kept the chickens. She could quickly dispatch, pluck and prepare a chicken and have it on the table in thirty minutes. Talk about fast food.

As Camp Leath grew in popularity and more motorists came through the gate, Myrtie Mae took advantage of the situation. She built cabins on the property, and she let out rooms in her house. In the 1930s, Camp Leath became Mount Air Camp, and in the '40s, there was the Mount Air Café, advertising "Milk Fed Chicken, White River Cat Fish and Steak Dinners with Salad, Vegetables and Home Made Pies." By this point, the chickens were no longer dispatched behind the place. Freshly rendered birds were brought from nearby Mount Air Farm twice a day. The restaurant became very well known for huckleberry pie.

Mount Air Camp, with its little shacks around a bathhouse and other facilities, in time became Mount Air Cottages, and in 1955, Jerry and

Above:
Mount
Air Camp.
*From historic
postcard.*

Left:
Blueberry
pancakes at
Myrtie Mae's
in Eureka
Springs.
Kat Robinson.

Opposite:
Inside Myrtie
Mae's in
Eureka
Springs.
Grav Weldon.

Martha Newton bought the camp and turned it into the Mount Air Court, replacing the cottages with a motor court in which every room was built into a strip of rooms and each guestroom had its own bathroom, with free TV in the rooms and a heated swimming pool to boot. Under David and Shirley Bird, the Mount Air Café restaurant became Country Kitchen in 1972. And in 1977, the Mount Air Court was franchised by the owners to a national motel chain, and the Best Western Inn of the Ozarks was born.

The restaurant came a long way from the days of Myrtie Mae's dining room table, but it never diverted from the cuisine she introduced to all those travelers. In 1992, the name of the restaurant was officially changed to Myrtie Mae's, which it's known as today. Folks still come in for that fried chicken and catfish, as well as a very hearty breakfast. The huckleberry pie is long gone, but it was replaced quite a long time back with a particularly Arkansas type of pie: the possum pie, a cream cheese pie with a pecan and flour crust, a whipped cream and pecan crown and chocolate custard in the middle.

Another of the great motor court hotels, the Sky Line Motel, is still around today as the Cottage Inn. Here, the individual cabins remain, refitted with modern amenities and Jacuzzi tubs. The COTTAGE INN RESTAURANT serves Mediterranean and French fare and has an extensive wine list.

1886 CRESCENT HOTEL

Even before Myrtie Mae Barrett was on the scene (and before she was born) there were tourists in Eureka Springs. They came for those healing waters (which, unlike those in Hot Springs, aren't thermal), and they came because they wanted to be well. Think about this: if it's the nineteenth century, you have enough money to go to a doctor and you have enough money for the train to get there, chances are you are rich enough to want to stay at the best place you can.

Enter the Crescent Hotel. The Frisco Railroad and the Eureka Improvement Company got together in 1884 to put up what they planned to be the most luxurious hotel in America. Roughly two years later, on May 20, 1886, the famed inn opened with much fanfare, including a gala ball, a banquet dinner and famous folks from all over.

For fifteen years, the hotel operated at the highest level of extravagance, sending footmen to fetch guests from the railroad, offering specialty services involving the springs—whatever it took. But that sort of service just wasn't sustainable, and the property began to fail. In 1908, it became the Crescent College and Conservatory for Young Women, which ran its course and closed in 1924. It was reopened as a junior college in 1930, but that only lasted for four years, after which it was leased out as a summer hotel.

The whole shebang was turned into a hospital in 1937 by new owner Norman Baker, a millionaire-inventor turned radio personality turned doctor with—I kid you not—no medical training whatsoever. He claimed he'd discovered cures for many ailments, including cancer, which, for the most part, was just drinking the mineral water from the area's springs.

Turns out "doctor" Baker had been run out of Iowa for doing something similar, and he was sent to jail in 1940 for mail fraud, for which he served four years. The hotel was purchased by four men in 1946, and it continued to operate until 1967, when a section of the fourth floor burned. There were efforts to fix it and keep it open, but eventually the Crescent was shuttered—that is,

The 1886 Crescent Hotel upon opening. *Courtesy 1886 Crescent Hotel.*

until 1997, when Marty and Elise Roenigk (the same couple who purchased War Eagle Mill) bought the old hotel and began a series of five stages of renovation. Today, the hotel is considered a top lodging option in the city, and it's known as the Most Haunted Hotel in America by many sources.

Through the changes and in every incarnation of ownership, the hotel hosted a restaurant. With the 1997 purchase and subsequent reopening, the 1886 Crystal Ballroom was refounded, serving absolutely amazing top-dollar dinners with traditional Victorian-style wait service. Recently, the evening service has been changed to the 1886 Steakhouse, with a more updated service style.

But what consistently draws guests both from this hotel and others is the famed Sunday brunch, combining breakfast specialties and omelets with hot dinner dishes, such as roast beef and pork loin, a selection of salads, marvelous desserts, a chocolate fountain and champagne—sometimes in the form of mimosas.

Even if you have concerns about staying in a haunted hotel, don't let it keep you from coming down for brunch on Sunday and enjoying this particular dining experience. You'll meet folks from all over the world who have come to Eureka Springs for everything it has to offer.

The good folks at the 1886 Crescent Hotel have allowed me to share this historic recipe.

HISTORIC MUFFINS
1886 CRESCENT HOTEL, EUREKA SPRINGS

Found in the *Ford Treasury of Favorite Recipes from Famous Eating Places*—published by the Ford Motor Company of Dearborn, Michigan, in 1950 and distributed locally by Crow Motor Company of Eureka Springs—was a recipe from the Crescent Hotel. The copy read as follows:

> *Crescent Hotel—Perched on the crest of the Ozark mountains, this resort hotel in the old tradition is surrounded by the hilly town of Eureka Springs. Breakfast [sic], lunch, and dinner served. Overnight accommodations and vacation facilities. Closed November 15 to April 1.*

1 cup huckleberries (blueberries can be substituted)
2 cups flour, plus ½ teaspoon
4 teaspoons baking powder
⅓ cup shortening
1 cup milk
1 egg, beaten

Wash and drain huckleberries and sprinkle with ½ teaspoon flour. Sift dry ingredients and cut in shortening. To this add milk and beaten egg. Stir in floured berries quickly; don't mash them. Pour a few tablespoons of batter into greased muffin tins. Bake for 20 minutes in a moderate (350-degree) oven. Pop a batch into the oven for a Sunday morning breakfast surprise.

DEVITO'S OF EUREKA SPRINGS

Back in 1956, a man by the name of Albert Raney started a trout farm. It was his second trout farm. The first was at a community once known as Wilcockson, not far north of Jasper. He diverted nearby Mill Creek to create a waterfall and pond on the property and renamed the community Marble Falls. The trout farm there eventually was sold in 1966 to the folks creating Dogpatch USA, which opened two years later.

The second trout farm, the one started in 1956, was at Bear Creek Springs north of Harrison. We'll get to talking about it and the restaurant that sprang up there shortly. There is this matter of family, though.

See, Mary Alice, Albert Raney's daughter, moved down to Little Rock to be a student at Baptist Hospital. And while she was down there, she met Jim DeVito. He was stationed at Camp Robinson in North Little Rock after World War II. DeVito was from Wisconsin by way of Illinois, but he liked it down here well enough. Mary Alice and Jim married in 1947, and they lived the army life, moving from station to station over the years.

In 1970, DeVito retired from the army, and they decided to move back to the Harrison area. Albert Raney decided to give them the trout farm to run and keep, which they did, along with Gene, Mary Alice's brother. They opened first an antique store and then, in 1986, a restaurant with their four boys. They did so well that in 1988, James DeVito, the oldest of Jim and Mary Alice's kids, opened his own place up in Eureka Springs.

James opened the new restaurant on Center Street about half a block from where it joins Spring Street at the Basin Park Hotel. Now, Italian joints have always been popular in the city, but the DeVito name also meant that fresh trout was always on the menu. Folks started sharing the word, and travelers would stop in for the signature dish, trout Italiano—boneless butterflied trout, sautéed in olive oil and garlic and topped with sautéed sweet peppers, capers and a touch of lemon. They'd stay for the excellent wine list and return time and time again for the homemade sauces and pastas and that amazing fresh bread.

In 2007, a lady by the name of Teresa Pelliccio moved to town. She took a job at DeVito's and became part of the community, and in 2010, she and James got married. These days, she hosts and bartends.

Business is going well. In 2012, the restaurant opened Sky Dining, an outdoor deck with a fantastic twist. See, thanks to Eureka Springs's rugged terrain, DeVito's opens right onto the street in the front and about three stories above Main Street on the back side. Now guests can dine above the fray below, with a delicious view to boot.

ERMILIO'S

Up above the downtown area, between two of Spring Street's many curves, you'll spot a small parking lot. And in that parking lot, you'll spot the Mona

Lamina. Bill Westerman's version of the Mona Lisa in tile has graced the lot for ages, and it bears the sign: "2005 Yard Art Award Winner Pro Division by Bill Westerman."

If the lot is empty, take a photo of the Mona Lamina and keep on moving. If the lot is full, chances are you are in for a wait, since Ermilio's Italian Home Cooking doesn't take reservations.

The house adjacent is two stories, Victorian in nature and usually packed between five and nine o'clock any night "in season." Put your name on the list, climb the stairs and have a glass of wine at the bar or sit out on the porch and watch the traffic of cars and carriages whiz by.

When you are seated, you're brought fresh bread and a whole clove of roasted garlic to smear on it. What follows is up to you; either you pair a pasta and a sauce or you choose a meat like chicken, steak or fish. It's simple and cozy, and when you're done, don't forget one of Jane's marvelous desserts.

BAVARIAN INN

Eureka Springs also boasts one of the few long-standing German restaurants in the state. The Bavarian Inn serves up German-Czech food in a chalet-style facility crisscrossed with heavy wooden beams, decorated with cuckoo clocks and loaded with a menu of sausages, cabbage and many things that are far better than the best sausage or cabbage.

The house specialty is half a roasted duck served in its own gravy, though you're just as likely to get the Bavarian Plate, with smoked pork, bratwurst, sauerkraut and herbed potato pancakes.

All that is well and good and reason enough to stop in for a meal. But what you really want, no matter how stuffed you are from your meal anywhere else, is to drop in and have apple strudel and coffee. The strudel is served hot on a fine china plate and has a wispy paper-thin, sugar-sprinkled crust that just embraces delectably spiced apples within. À la mode shouldn't even be an option—it's best with, of course.

Apple strudel at the Bavarian Inn in Eureka Springs. *Kat Robison.*

THE GRAND TAVERNE

Is there such a thing as casual elegant? Upscale comfort? There must be a word somewhere for the sort of atmosphere you find at the Grand Taverne.

The restaurant is housed in the historic Grand Central Hotel on Main Street. The building dates back to 1880 as the place where passengers first arrived after disembarking from trains from the North. In 1987, the facility was renovated top to bottom, suites were created for guests upstairs and a full-service spa and salon went in downstairs. The lobby, though, speaks of traditional Victorian charm; it's packed end to end with period furniture.

Inside the Grand Taverne in Eureka Springs. *Grav Weldon.*

The Grand Taverne spills out from its kitchen into this lobby. It's named after the very first full-menu service restaurant to offer table service: Le Grande Taverne de Londres, opened in 1782 in Paris. The name was chosen to convey a sense of attention to detail on food quality and service.

Its chef, Dave Gilderson, was schooled at L'Ecole de Cuisine Français Sabine de Mirbeck in England. He apprenticed in the south of France before returning to the States and working his way up through a number of assignments, including Branson's Big Cedar Lodge and his first stint as executive chef at the Candlestick Inn. Gilderson came to the Grand Central Hotel to open the Grand Taverne in 2003.

Chef Dave has become a community fixture, showing up at the farmers' market often and appearing at just about any sort of fundraising experience. He's put a board up on the sidewalk and writes something fanciful each night, and when you walk in, you can see what he did with the idea.

This is your fine dining experience, where you take your date when you're very serious about that person. The place is lit mostly by candlelight, with perfect wait service and cloth, silver and crystal. And if you're a connoisseur of fantastic food, you should consider the classic preparation of half duckling (blueberry citrus jus, dried cranberry wild rice)—a perfect duet of savory and sweet encompassing a marvelously prepared breast and leg of duck. And you have to get Chef Dave's Montrachet goat cheese cheesecake if it's offered—you just have to.

But here's the interesting thing. If you're lucky, there will be someone at the piano when you come in for dinner. And like as not, that person could be none other than Jerry Yester of the Lovin' Spoonful. He comes in often, regaling diners with renditions of the band's greatest hits, including "Do You Believe In Magic?" and, one of my favorites, "Summer in the City." And keep an ear open for one of his smart parodies.

SPARKY'S ROADHOUSE CAFÉ AND ULTRA LOUNGE

I first darkened the door at Sparky's Roadhouse Café and Ultra Lounge on the recommendation of Edwige Denyszyn, a lovely French woman who married Dr. Doug Hausler and started Keel's Creek Winery in town in the 2000s. I'd just attended a wine tasting and had hung around to chat. When I mentioned I wrote about food and travel, she chuckled, and when I asked her where she liked to eat, she told me she loved a place with good cheese. That place was this burger bar along U.S. 62.

And she's right. Sparky's isn't just a place where motorbikes pull up or where pool is played in dark rooms, though from the outside you might understand how one can get that impression. Within, Sparky's is a nice, comfortable, casual place that always feeds me well.

Yes, the burgers—a massive number of them—are fantastic, and the reddish cheese dip is one of my favorites. But that's not all the goodness served up at the popular red, white and black dive. There are fine dishes and common dishes and truffles, too. And the place is always open, even when it snows.

Wait, truffles? They are not the kind you find with a pig, but strongly alcoholic chocolate confections that are the perfect little dessert.

Owners David and Ruth Godwin-Hager first came to Eureka Springs in 1986. They both worked for David's sister Linda at the Cottage Inn; David cooked at the Plaza Restaurant, and Ruth worked for both Ermilio's and Bubba's. They opened Sparky's as a comfortable neighborhood hangout, with the café on one side with its 1950s décor and the Ultra Lounge cocktail bar and waiting area on the other.

By the way, Sparky's gets its name from a deceased and beloved pet of the Hagers.

One more tip: go use the restroom. For some strange reason, the folks who run Sparky's thought it'd be a great idea to decorate the women's restroom in less-than-classic album covers: *Banjo Spectacular!*, *String Along* with the Banjo Barons!, *All Star Color TV Revue*, Jimmy Peace Singers's *He Rescued Me*, *Music for Listening and Dancing*, the *Julie Andrews Christmas* album, *Caribbean Holiday* by the Gay Desperados Steel Orchestra, the Four Prep's less-than-popular *Dances and Dreaming* and Phil and Louis Palermo's *We Want to Sing*. Finally, we now know where bad LPs go to die.

BUBBA'S SOUTHERN PIT BARBECUE

The sign states, "It may not look famous, but it is." And that's what Bubba's Southern Pit Barbecue is to Eureka Springs. Bubba is Bob Wilson, who renovated an old building along U.S. 62 and moved into it with a pit for barbecuing all the way back in 1979.

Once you're parked and down the stairs, go find a seat at a table or a booth, if you can. The locals will be nice enough to crowd in a bit, but the tourists rarely are. That's all right; there's also a bar to sit at and takeout as well.

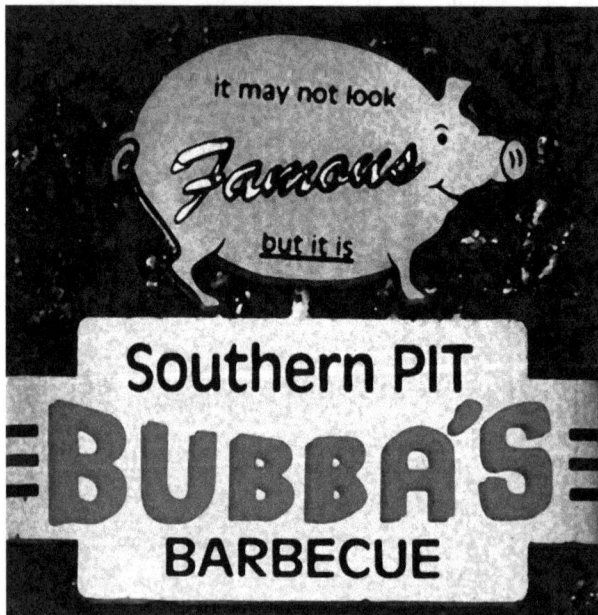

The sign at Bubba's Southern Pit Barbecue in Eureka Springs. *Kat Robinson.*

The nachos—piled high with cheese, lettuce, tomatoes, avocado and jalapeño pepper slice and topped with pork, beef or chicken from the pit—are legendary. There's a bean version for non–meat eaters and an industrial-strength version that kicks it up a notch with homemade chili atop those fresh, fried corn tortilla chips. GET RIBS. Folks rave on the pulled pork shoulder and the brisket. GET RIBS. The burger's pretty good and the coleslaw some of the best you'll find in the area, but GET RIBS.

LOCAL FLAVOR CAFÉ

If Eureka Springs has a heart to its culinary scene, it has to be Local Flavor Café. Opened in 1991, the restaurant has grown both culinarily and exponentially, consuming an entire lot above Main Street close to the Aud.

The original restaurant was started by Janice and Kirby Murray in what had been an art studio/gallery/residence known as KJ's Creations. Before that, the place had been the local Christian Science Reading Room.

Local Flavor started out as a coffeehouse that offered a few pastries and sandwiches. It passed through several sets of hands, going in 1997 from Janice to Rick Gullege and Jim MacAvey, who had a dream about having their own little place in town, and then to Britt Evans, who had worked for all of them.

Britt's a multigenerational native, with family who settled in the area way back in 1820. Six generations in, he comes by cooking naturally. When he was a young boy, he'd pull a chair up to the stove when his grandparents were cooking and ask questions. He was five years old when they started letting him cook. He started with the small things—eggs, hamburger—he had a play restaurant on the back porch with an old camp stove, kitchen table and a couple chairs, and he'd pretend he had customers coming in.

Britt's mom, Brenda, has been involved in the food service industry in town all her life. She was one of the owners of Brenda and Lanta's on Center Street for a few years there. That restaurant became Center Street Café and then Center Street South of the Border, owned by Clary Perez and KJ Zumwalt, of the previously mentioned KJ's Creations. After KJ moved Center Street out to U.S. 62 and renamed the business KJ's Caribe, the space became home to The Squid and The Whale, a local pub.

Britt's first stint at Local Flavor came in 1992. The next year, he set off to go out of town. He'd been in Denver about five years and was wanting

The Mexican Scramble at Local Flavor Café in Eureka Springs. *Kat Robinson.*

to relocate. He also wanted to go to the New England Culinary Institute up in Vermont, so he needed to stick some money back. So back to Eureka Springs he came in 1998, picking up three or four jobs to get through and earn some savings. He waited tables at Local Flavor and Ermilio's and did some construction here and there.

What he wasn't planning on was what Jim and Rick offered. They'd only been in the place just over a year and realized that running a restaurant together really wasn't their dream after all. Britt had a plan, though. He was going to cook his way around the world and decide what he wanted to do from there when he finally returned. Well, you can't find an opportunity like what was dropped in his lap every day, so two weeks later, he bought Local Flavor. On August 14, 1998, it was his.

"Once I started thinking of the opportunity that was right in front of me—it was a very reasonable purchase price, they just didn't want to do it any more—I couldn't pass it up. I feel we're all put on this earth to complete a task we're meant to do."

At first, Britt kept one of the other jobs, knocking out breakfast and lunch at Local Flavor and then waiting tables over at Ermilio's for owner Paul Wilson. He admits he wanted to fine tune his chops and get in as much knowledge as possible. It had to be a killer schedule, though.

Eventually, Britt decided to tackle dinner, and at that point, mom Brenda—working at DeVito's at the time—quit there and came on board. Brenda Evans worked there until she retired in 2012. "It's always been a great asset to me to have someone so trustworthy in my corner, on my side, and to get to spend so much time working with someone you love and adore is just this great thing," Britt told me, unashamed.

Britt inherited Rick and Jim's menu and slowly put his mark on it. That's saying a lot, considering the restaurant he inherited had a kitchen that was just ten by twelve feet. Today, that kitchen is, quote, "a monster." As the clientele has grown, so has the restaurant. Britt balances it out. When the restaurant seems to need room to seat folks waiting, he's expanded the dining areas. When the wait for food has lengthened, he's expanded the kitchen. There's nowhere left to expand to now—every inch of the lot is taken up with the building today, and there's even a patio that slightly overhangs Main Street.

Today, the menu is distinctive, and it truly reflects the flavors of Eureka Springs. Britt is married with two kids—his wife is a decorator, who created the look at Local Flavor—and he still lives by a certain idea that's served him well:

"From the day I opened, my business hasn't been about margins and penny-pinching and saving and squeezing the life out of my staff. We think about the guest first in everything we do. In doing that, we've never had to worry about the money."

KJ's Caribe

Building on the love you share with someone can be one of the greatest experiences of your life. But what happens when one part of that equation is lost?

One answer can be found at KJ's Caribe Restaurant y Cantina. Caribe (as everyone calls it) is out west of downtown on Highway 62, a brightly decorated building, colored in every shade of the rainbow and oozing art. It's a beautiful place to meet and chill. It's also a remembrance.

The original restaurant was opened downtown by KJ Zumwalt and Clary Perez back in 1992. Clary was the cook; KJ worked the front of the house. They had a beautiful partnership. Clary's Panamanian food brought them loyal and friendly customers both among the locals and among those who (like me) come up on a regular basis to enjoy the town.

Clary was born to a wealthy family in Panama. Her parents sent her to school in Cullman, Alabama, in 1961, and after graduation, she moved to New York City's Greenwich Village. She found her way to the Arco Iris community in 1978 and moved to nearby Eureka Springs a short time later. KJ came to town in 1989 with, as she says, "a bad attitude and an overnight bag" to stay for three days, and she never left. They met, and it was beautiful. KJ was up front, warming customers with her effervescent attitude. Clary brought her native dishes out and won over the hearts of a community.

Sadly, some time back, KJ lost Clary. Rather than move on to another place or business, KJ did everything for the eatery they built together to succeed. She moved to the back of the house, cooking all the great food from Clary's recipes and keeping her alive through that great food. She moved the restaurant in 2002, away from oppressively high downtown rents and into the building that she could eventually own outright. And every night, she cooks.

Four nights a week (Thursday through Sunday), KJ is in the kitchen with her sous chef and her dishwasher, turning out one dish after another. She's like no other chef I've ever met. When I met her she was wearing a little black dress, a black apron and pink cowboy boots. And she was vivacious as all hell.

Outside chili cook-offs and barbecue joints, I've never seen anyone else wear cowboy boots in a kitchen. But KJ dances. In her long kitchen with its large windows and every color of the rainbow on the walls, she dances, whipping up guacamole and sautéing shrimp and bringing together dishes that are causes for celebration.

Inside KJ's Caribe in Eureka Springs. *Grav Weldon*.

Clary Perez. *Photo courtesy KJ Zumwalt, image courtesy Grav Weldon.*

Her signature item, the Center Street Salsa Platter, is seven concoctions for dipping served up in an oyster dish. The sauces are a hot sweet mango pepper salsa, a red bell pepper pico, a green tomato pico, a pineapple pico, sour cream, a fresh tomato salsa and a chutney-like tomatillo cilantro concoction.

KJ once pointed out to me the sauces' deep tones on the white plate. "You see the green?" she asked and pointed at her eyes. "The lipstick salsa? It's all about the love."

I do see it. Clary's recipes captured KJ's green eyes and red lips, dollops of paint on a canvas of a beautiful partnership that continues over time and space, profound and absolute.

KJ's guacamole. *Grav Weldon.*

Passion. You know, you hear the word batted around on these TV shows, but **KJ** embodies it. Her food embodies it. Each flavor in the salsa platter punches through bright and clean and unique, especially on the flour and corn chips fried fresh each day. It shows in the remarkable turkey leg mole (you know you are a true friend when she grants you a jar of her splendid mole sauce). It shows in the huge mound of fresh guacamole, piled on spinach leaves in an oversized margarita glass and topped with tiny bits of tomatoes, spicy and rich and fresh.

And it shows up in what she does outside the restaurant. She's intricately involved in this small hill-bound community. Everyone knows her. She's out fundraising here and there, standing up for causes and running pell-mell down Spring Street in those cowboy boots in the annual Waiters' Race during the Fleur Delicious Festival. As I said, she dances, and the eatery she continues to nurture reinforces that through its flavors and the influences it continues to have on the cuisine of a community.

When I asked for recipes for this book, she responded in a flash, almost as quickly as I'd asked. Her contribution is a party-sized rendition of that marvelous guacamole.

GUACAMOLE FOR A BIG PARTY
KJ's CARIBE, EUREKA SPRINGS

3 Spanish yellow onions
1 bulb garlic
9 serrano peppers
20 Haas avocados
3 tablespoons garlic powder
2 tablespoons sea salt
1 tablespoon cayanne
2 limes

Mince the onions, garlic and serrano peppers. Gently mash avocados in, and then, very lightly and carefully, stir in the spices. Squeeze two limes over the guacamole. Serve over greens and sprinkle with diced red bell pepper or tomato.

Chapter 9

U.S. 65 THROUGH THE HEART
OF THE ARKANSAS OZARKS

*In the space of one hundred and seventy-six years the Lower Mississippi has
shortened itself two hundred and forty-two miles. This is an average of a trifle
over one mile and a third per year. Therefore, any calm person, who is not blind or
idiotic, can see that in the Old Oolitic Silurian Period, just a million years ago next
November, the Lower Mississippi River was upward of one million three hundred
thousand miles long, and stuck out over the Gulf of Mexico like a fishing-rod. And
by the same token any person can see that seven hundred and forty-two years from
now the Lower Mississippi will be only a mile and three-quarters long, and Cairo
and New Orleans will have joined their streets together, and be plodding comfortably
along under a single mayor and a mutual board of aldermen.*
Mark Twain
Life on the Mississippi

U.S. Highway 65 runs over 300 miles from the Louisiana border to
the Missouri border, passing from the soft, flat soil of the Delta up
through the Ozarks. The stretch that runs from Conway to just south
of Ridgedale, Missouri, is about 127 miles today, but it used to be a lot,
lot further.

Back when the route was first created in 1926, it was assembled out of
sections of existing roadway patched together all through the region. South
of Little Rock, this was no problem, since once the rolling hills smooth out
into the Delta Plain, the road could sit alongside the established railway. But
starting with the trek into the Ozarks at Conway, it was a matter of matching

paths and dirt roads from one community to another. U.S. 65 doglegged and jagged back and forth like a jitterbugging goat.

I think I might have first made the drive up 65 around the age of six or seven. It might have been going to Dogpatch USA or to Branson or to visit family. What I remember is that it took forever. Once we turned off I-40 at Conway, it'd take hours to get as far as Clinton, Leslie or Harrison. The two-lane highway was sacked with curves, hills, sharp angles and a lot of local drivers.

The bypassing started in the south and moved north. Conway's growing population and suburban sprawl meant a four-lane route was needed and a turn lane to boot. Truckers found the road the shortest distance between Springfield and Little Rock, and in keeping up with the traffic, there was a defined need to widen the road as well. The need for climbing lanes and even a runaway truck ramp (between Dennard and Leslie) was determined. The Arkansas Highway and Transportation Department chipped away at each hurdle and started the northern expansion of the route. Just in my lifetime, bypasses have made the route fourteen miles shorter.

Today, the road is four lanes all the way to the north side of Damascus, with four-lane sections built at Clinton and Marshall. Harrison is also a four-lane bypass, all the way up to the Missouri state line (including one pair of bridges that stand two hundred feet above the valley below).

But it's come at a cost. Little communities like Omaha and Western Grove are now mostly cut off from the main highway, and Bear Creek Springs has been bypassed twice. The little towns survive or don't, and those that don't are eventually lost to history.

More than a dozen sections in these counties are now signed Old 65, and even some of those spurs lack a connection to the newer road. The need to cut through mountains has made a formerly long drive between Damascus and Greenbrier into a short jaunt and separated former next-door neighbors Coursey's Smoked Meats and Ferguson's Country Store in St. Joe.

But the route's abbreviation in length is outclassed by the speeds now allowed. With better-quality roadbeds and more multilane sections, you can now make it to Harrison from Conway in around two hours, since the only stoplights along that route are in Greenbrier, Clinton and Marshall. No longer does the highway traverse downtowns.

The changes can be seen as progress, but it's interesting to note that most of the restaurants in this chapter have survived because they are on sections of U.S. 65 that remain on the same route today.

Still, under that idea from Mark Twain, if I've been heading up and down U.S. 65 in some way or another for thirty years and it's gone from 141 miles to 127 miles from Conway to the border in that time, you should be able to make the drive in, what, less than an hour in the next century?

DeVito's Italian Restaurant

Back in the days when U.S. 65 was two lanes of twists, turns, inclines and declines spanning half a state, it was also a hallway for businesses and attractions. On its curves, it held rock shops, quilt stores, smokehouses, fruit stands and every sort of visually appealing sight. There were places to stop to view grand vistas, little quaint towns with old manned service stations, bluffs and waterfalls along roadsides and cute country-clad motels. And at one place, there was a trout farm.

Bear Creek Spring's section of U.S. 65 was partially bypassed in 1982, with a slight easterly repositioning of the right of way about a block off the original path. A few years ago, a second bypass took the road even further to the east, and the valley that contains the spring and its creek has quieted down.

There are still some of the signs from the original alignment of the highway along the stretch, and there's still a trout farm and a restaurant there, which draws thousands down into the hollow each year. It's the home of the DeVito family.

The fifth generation of DeVito cooks are still preparing some of the best Italian specialties you can find in Arkansas.

I mentioned earlier about Albert Raney and his trout farm and daughter Mary Alice, who went to North Little Rock to go to school at Baptist Hospital and came back to Harrison with an army serviceman nearly three decades later. And I've already talked about one of their four sons, James, who runs the second DeVito's in Eureka Springs with his wife, Teresa. Of course, that came later.

In 1970, upon arriving back in the Harrison area, Albert Raney gave his daughter and son-in-law the trout farm at Bear Creek Springs. Located just a frog's spit from U.S. 65, it drew families who loved the trout experience, especially since, being a privately owned creek, it didn't require anyone to get a fishing license to drop a line in and pull out a fish.

It was fun and quick and the result was trout, a "take-and-make" meal of the utmost freshness.

But the first bypass in 1982 proved the adage "out of sight, out of mind." Fewer folks whizzing past to head to Branson or Harrison stopped in to cast their reels. Business shrank. Still, the family survived, placing new signs out on the road and encouraging what business they could bring in.

And they had another idea. They already had an antique shop going across the street from the trout farm. They had the building, and they had a second story to work with. So in 1986, with the four boys back home from college and full partners in the enterprise, the DeVitos opened a restaurant across the road from the trout farm. It became an overnight success. People would drive in for miles around to come eat fresh trout and fabulous Italian dishes in the little restaurant over the antique store and rock shop. Some would come and fish at the farm and have their catches cooked up fresh, but far more came just to eat and experience a fabulous Italian experience in the Ozarks.

The popularity was well earned. The men—Jim and sons James, Steve, Chris and Joe—held court in the kitchen, cooking fish and making sides, bread and dessert from scratch. Their rich, tomato-strong sauce became famous, as did their overstuffed ravioli. The restaurant drew in business so fast that two years after opening oldest son James picked up and started that second restaurant in Eureka Springs, which was also an instant hit. And in the late 1990s, a third DeVito's was opened at Big Cedar Lodge near Branson.

That last restaurant was fortuitous. In 2000, DeVito's original restaurant at Bear Creek Springs was destroyed by fire. Business still continued at Big Cedar Lodge, but there was a decision to be made. Brothers Steve, Chris and Joe knew they had to rebuild. Fourteen months later, they were open once again, in a beautiful new facility that was twice as large as the old one. It thrived from the moment its doors opened.

But the highway wasn't done with DeVito's. The late "oughts" (or whatever you'd like to call the 2000s) brought controversy to folks all along the Harrison–Branson corridor, with the coming of a four-lane replacement for the major highway that connected the two cities. The new road was given the U.S. 65 designation; the old road became a series of local loops along the way, and DeVito's restaurant and trout farm were that much further from the hubbub of traffic.

Still, the word's gotten out about DeVito's. It's now considered one of the top dining spots in the county, and it's the place to take your most important dates. The new liquor license in 2011 has certainly helped. And when it comes to the staff, the restaurant is full of DeVitos, including the sixth and eventually seventh generations.

The springs are as they always were, clear and a constant fifty-eight degrees year round. It's full of rainbow trout, ranging from small fry to buggers in the five-pound range. You can still go down and fish, and you can take home whatever you catch, cleaned and packed in ice at the bargain rate of $6.25 a pound. Now, though, you can also pay an extra $8.00 and get that trout cooked and served up with a choice of potato, hush puppies or a salad.

Grav and I went out there one warm Sunday morning in April 2011. Joe DeVito showed us across the old footbridge and down to the westernmost pool, where we could see trout popping the water and nosing up to the bank. They're used to people; fish feed is available for a quarter a handful to toss in. Kids love to watch the feeding frenzy.

"We had four really big ones in that pool over there," Joe points out as we walked along, "but an otter got them."

No matter. We sat down our bag and inspected the tackle we'd brought along. I cast out first, getting a hit right off the bat on a piece of fish food from a small fish, maybe a half pound in size. Joe came over and unhooked the little one and tossed him back in.

"I remember passing by here as a kid. I think I even fished out here a few times," I told Joe. I couldn't quite pin the memory down for certain, but I did recall coming out with my best friend in the early 1990s to cast out a line or two. When I was a kid, there would be days when kids would be lined up all along the bank, nearly shoulder to shoulder. Sometimes people would have to wait.

"And it's always been this way?"

"People used to come out all the time and catch their dinner. But since the highway moved in '82, it hasn't been as busy."

I pulled in my first keeper of the day, a pounder who'd swallowed the treble hook on my spoon. Joe expertly flicked it off and dropped it into water in a wire box at the water's edge. I pulled out two more that were in the pound-and-a-half range as Grav caught shots across the pond. Then it was his turn.

I took the camera, and he made his first unsuccessful cast. Maybe I shouldn't have poked fun, but on his next cast, he hooked on quick to something with some fight to it. For several minutes, it pulled back on him, wearing itself out. Joe joined him on the bank with the net, and together they pulled out a two-and-a-half-pound beauty.

Trout from the DeVito's trout farm (and Grav's shoe). *Grav Weldon.*

It was still fighting and managed to get off the hook onto the bank. Joe picked it up, took it over to the fishing shed and deftly bonked it on the head with a short metal rod. The fish quieted, and I got to shoot my photographer with his catch.

A few minutes later, he hooked in again, this time bringing in a three-and-a-half-pounder. I felt duly humbled at my earlier success.

I cast in again while he took fish pictures. It was funny to watch him as he took off a shoe and placed it next to the fish on the bank. His three-and-a-half pounder was longer than his size twelve and a half loafer. I had one more catch that day, a two pounder, my largest. And that was it, enough fish for dinner and to take home to smoke for later. The entire operation had taken less than ten minutes.

We talked with Joe as he took our catch into the shed and ran water in a sink. He told us about growing up with the trout farm as he expertly beheaded and gutted the fish one by one. They were each cleaned thoroughly and put in a container. He then took the largest of the fish and carefully butterflied it as we watched.

"It took me a while to learn this," he said. "When we just had the trout farm, we'd just clean them and pack them away. Now, some folks cook them whole with the bones in them. I think people like it better when there aren't any bones in them."

He slid the knife along one side of the ribcage and then the other and removed it, then slid it into the meat on each side and removed the second row of bones. A quick trim of the belly fat and there was a gorgeous butterflied fillet of trout.

He filleted two more, and then we were heading back across the footbridge.

Such is a stop on a good day at DeVito's. Usually, it's the kids you see down by the creek, but sometimes, you might catch sight of a well-dressed woman or a man in a suit, seeing what she or he can pull out.

And when you take it in, you have the option of so many methods of preparation: charbroiled with Cajun seasoning, broiled with a cream sauce, dipped in cornmeal and fried, covered in a sweet basil and garlic pesto, deep fried and slathered in a toasted almond butter sauce or prepared with house seasoning. And they're all good, in my opinion.

There are other choices, like the appetizers. The trout fingers are likely the best known—smaller pieces of trout, cornmeal battered and perfect for dipping. Toasted ravioli comes out hand-packed with Parmesan and mozzarella and tiny slivers of salami, with a tomato and pork-dripping marinara. There's another ravioli that's chicken and spinach and cheese, and there's Italian stuffed bread.

And of course, there are the pastas. The family still makes all the pasta and sauces, and they come in many varieties: ravioli, spaghetti, fettuccini, egg noodles and angel hair. There are steaks. And then there are desserts—usually Steve's realm there—and always there's at least one sort of pie.

Folks come back. They come back again and again and again. There's a vegetarian couple who came in every night and several times a week for lunch and always chose an order of eggplant parmigiano to share, every week right up until the guy passed away. Some folks are local regulars, and some, like me, make a point of stopping in when they're in town. I always get something with the half order of fettuccini Alfredo—I love their Alfredo sauce—and I always ask for a little extra bread.

Up on the old highway, the signs still point into the hollow. And out on the new four-lane, there's a sign that says just where to turn to head down to the trout farm. If you're along the way, it's worth a stop. Don't worry if you forgot your fishing pole—they have tackle you can borrow.

The family sent along the recipe for the bourbon chocolate pecan pie for this book. It is absolutely incredible.

BOURBON CHOCOLATE PECAN PIE
DeVito's Italian Restaurant, Bear Creek Springs

1 homemade pie crust, or ½ (15-ounce) package
   refrigerated pie crust
4 large eggs
1 cup light corn syrup
6 tablespoons butter or margarine, melted
½ cup sugar
¼ cup firmly packed light brown sugar
3 tablespoons bourbon
1 tablespoon all-purpose flour
1 teaspoon vanilla extract
1 cup coarsely chopped pecans
1 cup (6 ounces) semisweet chocolate morsels

Heat oven to 350 degrees.
   Fit pie crust into a nine inch pie plate. Fold edges under and crimp.
   *Whisk together eggs and next seven ingredients until mixture
is smooth. Stir in pecans and morsels. Pour into pie crust.*
   Bake on lowest oven rack for one hour, until set.

Bourbon chocolate pecan pie at DeVito's Italian Restaurant at Bear Creek Springs. *Kat Robinson.*

MASTER CHEF

South of where U.S. 62 and U.S. 65 converge (today, above Bear Creek Springs, at what's now known as the Eureka Springs overpass), the highway goes through town. Today's path takes it almost to the downtown area before making a hard left at a stoplight and out onto two successive loops of bypass.

Before the bypass, the highways converged with Arkansas Highway 7 and rolled into downtown as Main Street. Along this stretch you'll find the offices for local radio stations, a handful of old motor courts and roadside hotels (some of which are still in operation), shops and even the grand Hotel Seville. Main Street hits the downtown square a couple blocks later, on which sits the grand restored Lyric Theater. After a couple blocks more, Highway 7 splits and goes south, while U.S. 65B crosses the bridge over little Harrison Lake and heads into the older suburbs.

Not far from where the north end of the bypass hooks in, you'll find a red-roofed restaurant that's been hanging around serving the town—and traffic to Dogpatch USA—since 1969. This is Master Chef.

This is not a fine dining establishment with a culinary-schooled chef and white-glove service. This is a community diner with an eclectic menu that's been around for nearly forty-five years.

Master Chef served up what the community wanted and needed: another dairy diner. But then something interesting happened. Someone would come in and ask for a dish, and the folks there would attempt to make it. And if it was good, it got added to the menu. So over the years, the menu broadened. There were Ark-Mex dishes like the plato de saltillo (saltillo plate, an enchilada covered in red sauce, cheese taco covered in cheese sauce, beef taco in a hard shell and tortilla chips with salsa, a long-standing popular combination at many Arkansas Mexican restaurants), fried chicken, cold sandwiches, barbecue sandwiches, shrimp dinners, fried catfish, "diet-centered meals," fajita plates and even cashew chicken (the latter of which is less surprising when you learn that this popular "Chinese" dish was created just over an hour away in Springfield, Missouri). Baked potatoes stuffed with ham? All right. Raisin fried pie? Sure, why not?

What's crazy about Master Chef is that items kept going on the menu, and they didn't come off.

I can remember visiting the restaurant on one of those Dogpatch USA trips as a kid. Even then, I can recall coming in, walking through the waist-high divided lobby and up to the ordering counter and being absolutely overwhelmed by the choices. On visiting in April 2011, when I looked up

Chicken fingers at Master Chef in Harrison. *Kat Robinson.*

and my eyes got big at the even more expanded menu above the kitchen, the counter girl handed me a three ring binder full of items to choose from.

Ron and Burlene Hinson bought Master Chef in 1992 from Jerry Sharp. Burlene had worked at Master Chef since it opened in 1969; she knew what made the restaurant great, and she didn't change a thing. The Hinsons have kept up the long-established business and it's still a very important part of the community.

So Master Chef does a lot of things, but does it do them well? The Ark-Mex is good—it's not the authentic Mexican fare we're used to today, but it's not expected to be, either. Burgers are fine, and the stuffed potatoes are pretty dang good. And then there are the chicken strips. I suppose at some point, someone came in and suggested that since Master Chef did fried chicken, it should also offer fried chicken strips. Rather than ordering a box of prebreaded pieces to throw in a deep fryer, the strips there are actually hand-pulled strips of breast delicately battered and spiced. It still looks like chicken, rather than another battered and deep-fried wonder.

COURSEY'S SMOKED MEATS

The highway's course, as I mentioned, has changed a lot through the years. I understand the need for expediency, I most certainly do. And I understand why it's important to change the routes of highways built over Native American paths, postal routes and dirt roads over time to make them safer. But I will never understand why the Arkansas Highway and Transportation Department decided to take U.S. 65 and relocate it between Coursey's Smoked Meats and Ferguson's Country Store on the south side of St. Joe.

The two restaurants have been around for ages on the first ridge north of the Buffalo National River. Coursey's opened in 1945, and Ferguson's started in 1973. For the longest time, they were the perfect one-two punch on the right side of the road, the best place to fuel up and use the restroom before heading north. The two shops were also the best place along the route, in my opinion, to pick up gifts to take home—smoked meats and jellies, quilts and handcrafts and, of course, cinnamon rolls for the ride.

Lynn Coursey spent his life as a gourmet chef. He moved back to St. Joe when he retired, at the end of World War II, and set up shop on the unpaved road that went through the county. He wanted to do something that would give him a chance to speak to people, and what better way than by capitalizing on postwar travelers taking their cars out on treks in the Ozarks?

Lynn Coursey's hams were prepared in an old, dirt-floored log smokehouse (which still stands today out front of the more modern shop). He would take a ham, salt and tie it, put a nail in the wall and tie that ham to

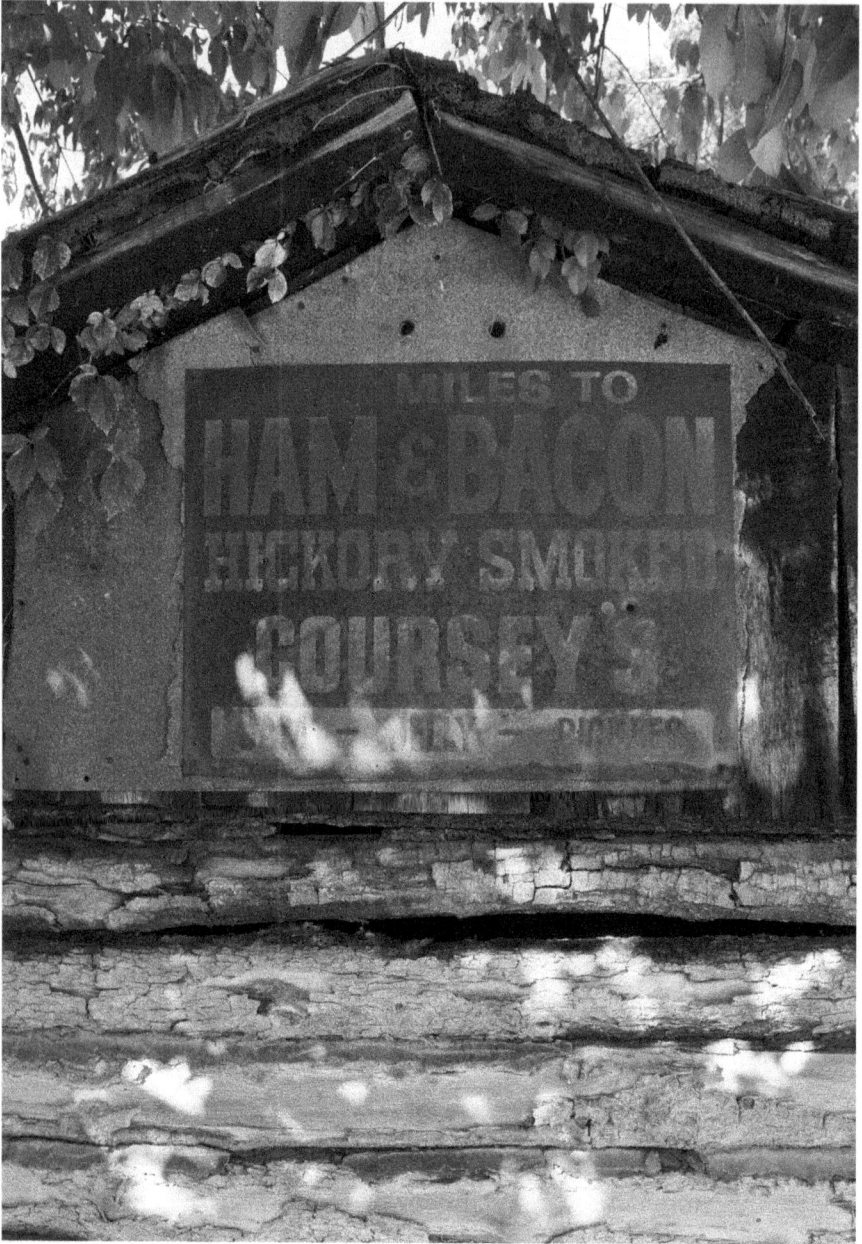

Coursey's Smoked Meats sign at the store in St. Joe. *Grav Weldon.*

it. There's not a whole lot of difference between what he did then and what the family does now.

Today, Coursey's Smoked Meats is managed by Mary Lu Coursey, his granddaughter. There are two generations after that as well. They still smoke hams, along with bacon (it's pretty famous), turkey and summer sausage, as well as swiss and cheddar cheeses. They also sell jams and jellies. Most folks get their meat by the pound, sliced and wrapped when it's ordered. But you can also take home a whole country ham. If you want a hearty belly laugh, read Jane and Michael Stern's *Two for the Road: Our Love Affair with American Food*. Turn to page 137. Trust me on this.

FERGUSON'S COUNTRY STORE AND RESTAURANT

Ferguson's started life a little differently. The big two-story structure on top of the hill was the creation of Jim and Scottie Ferguson, who wanted to build a place where local artisans could share their crafts. The old stone and natural lumber gives the place an American lodge–style feel, but it's authentic. Artists made the special chandeliers in the place from old wagon and cultivar wheels.

Ferguson's also sold handcrafted furniture, and there was a whole warehouse out back full of tables, chairs and bedsteads. The same tables and chairs were used inside the building for the restaurant that thrived there.

The Fergusons gave the property to the North Arkansas Community College Foundation in 1986, which then sold the place to Wayne and Peggy Thompson for the money to build a new library. The Thompsons have stuck with the idea, providing not only great breakfasts and lunches to passersby but also a great place for craftsmen and quilters to sell their wares. They have also become great folks to turn to in the community around the Buffalo National River.

There used to be a billboard on U.S. 65, advertising Ferguson's giant cinnamon rolls as "almost actual size." They are pretty big—about five inches square. When you order one in the store, it comes out on a plate by itself (I doubt anyone ever orders two) covered in icing. When you get one to go, it comes in a single Styrofoam box with a whole cup of icing. And it's good.

Inside Ferguson's Country Store and Restaurant in St. Joe. *Kat Robinson*.

THE ROUTE TO LITTLE ROCK

I have friends and family all over Arkansas, and one side of my brother's family comes from Searcy County. So I have been familiar with the DAISY QUEEN since my adolescence. The little dairy shack on the east side of Highway 65 in Marshall has received a little facelift here and there over the years, but it's still serving up burgers, shakes and all the things a little community like Marshall might want to eat.

Each community along the way has its places to eat. A large ridge to the south of town separates Marshall from points south. U.S. 65 crosses it directly in the middle, and there's a great lookout on top where you can see close to forever. On the other side, Leslie has several places that have opened in the past decade in its downtown off the highway. MISTY'S SHELL before the turn-off does diner-style breakfasts and Saran-wrapped fried pies. On the far side, there's SERENITY FARMS BAKERY, which, in addition to doing marvelous breads and focaccias, also provides bread to several places in Central Arkansas, including the Whole Foods in Little Rock.

Daisy Queen in Marshall. *Kat Robinson.*

And further down, between Clinton and Bee Branch, you'll find the CHUCK WAGON RESTAURANT. This little place has changed hands a couple times over the years, but it serves a mean chicken-fried steak. And there's always a fantastic pie in the case.

Chapter 10

U.S. 62 ACROSS THE TOP OF ARKANSAS

On the other side of Harrison, U.S. 62 and U.S. 65 go their separate ways. U.S. 62 bounds off to the east for 103 miles before meeting U.S. 167 at Ash Flat. Today, it's a pretty straight shot that includes a bypass of Mountain Home, but until the 1980s, it had significant delays along its route in the form of ferries.

River crossings have always been part of the passage. U.S. 62's course takes it across the White River, the North Fork, the Strawberry, the Spring and the Black, as well as a number of creeks. The first major ferry replacement on the route happened in 1930 with the construction of the Ruthven Bridge (commonly known as the Rainbow Bridge) at Cotter. The Smith Ferry ran at the North Fork River until 1934, when a concrete bridge was opened at Henderson. This bridge was inundated in 1943, though, with waters filling Norfork Lake, and wasn't superseded until a new bridge was opened in the 1980s. The 1934 Henderson bridge now sits eighty feet below the surface.

In the intervening years, the Panther Bay ferry ran. Known as the "Arkansas Navy," this was the only passage for miles, and it carried not only U.S. 62 across the lake to the east but Arkansas Highway 101 to the north.

The section of road to the east of Norfork Lake all the way to Ash Flat wasn't completely paved until 1958.

The restaurants that managed to make it before the promise of that new crossing in the 1980s are slim, with just a few holdouts. But after the bridge opening, the area blossomed with new dining options, and Mountain Home in particular flourished.

Highway 62 & 101 Ferry, Panther Bay Landing, Lake Norfork, Arkansas

Historic postcard of the Panther Bay Ferry. *Boston Public Library.*

Past Ash Flat, U.S. 62 runs up through Cherokee Village to Hardy and then over to Pocahontas, where from the ridge of downtown, you can see the beginnings of the long flat plain that forms the Arkansas Delta.

THE VILLAGE WHEEL AND THE 178 CLUB

The city of Bull Shoals was founded in 1954 on the last peninsula into the newly formed Bull Shoals Lake. Its location restricts its growth, which is just fine for folks who have located to the area for its great fishing and small-town atmosphere.

There aren't a lot of restaurants in the burg, but two of them are worthy of mention. One is The Village Wheel. Danette Stubenfoll and Cindy Stubenfoll Crosslin's restaurant is a gathering place for families, especially in the morning. Breakfasts at the three-decade-old restaurant are hearty, and the place has become very well known for its desserts, listed on a whiteboard each day, usually a variety of homemade cakes and pies. There's also a great gift shop attached.

The 178 Club takes its name from the highway that rolls through town. It's anything but a normal club. Open since 1980, it's the only place I know

The 178 Club in Bull Shoals. *Grav Weldon*.

of in Arkansas where you can enjoy fine dining and pick up a spare as well. See, it's also the local bowling alley.

While many alleys have snack bars, the 178 Club is truly top-of-the-line dining, with fantastic steaks, baked Brie and escargot. The burgers bear names like "The Strike," "The Split" and "The Gutter." And the restaurant's one of those few where you can bring in your catch of the day and have it prepared for you, complete with soup, salad and all the fixings.

GASTON'S RESTAURANT

Cross Bull Shoals Dam and head below it down to the White River for one of the oldest restaurants in the area. Al Gaston bought the little resort with just six cabins and six boats back in 1958. Since then, the place has expanded exponentially and now boasts seventy-nine cabins, more than seventy boats, an airstrip, a swimming pool, a private club, nature trails and a popular restaurant.

Inside Gaston's Restaurant. *Grav Weldon.*

Championship pies at Nima's Pizza in Gassville. *Courtesy Nima's Pizza.*

Gaston's Restaurant sits right over the White River, with a bank of large windows overlooking the water. Overhead, there's everything from bicycles to boat motors, and the oversized salad bar and buffet is organized within the frame of an old johnboat. The dish of the day is White River rainbow trout, served up in so many ways: broiled, steamed, fried, almandine, with mushrooms, hollandaise or in poppers. But the star could very well be the steak Neptune—a broiled rib-eye, smothered in crab, prawns and mushrooms and topped with béarnaise sauce.

NIMA'S PIZZA

On the other side of the famed Cotter Bridge, past the Cotter community, you'll find Gassville and a little pizzeria that's claiming big honors.

Nima's Pizza opened in the 1990s and served its community well. In 2003, it was purchased from its original owners by a Las Vegas couple, and within a few years, it gained international notoriety. Rick and Jane Miles loved visiting the Mountain Home area and decided to retire there, as well as purchase Nima's with no restaurant experience. They learned, though, and utilized a collection of premium aged cheeses, oils from the Devo Olive Oil

Company in Branson and recipes that required a wait—doughs that take more than a day, well-developed sauces and four-hour roasted peppers.

It paid off in a big way in 2010, when Jane and Rick took their pizzas back to Las Vegas for the International Pizza Challenge. They came home with the title of #2 Best World Traditional Pizza, right behind a chef out of Italy.

They've proved it's no fluke, with good showings over the past few years and another #2 in 2013. The winning pie for this past contest was a simple one baked on a day-rise crust, with a layer of thin sliced black pepper–laced Italian ham covered by a light sauce and then a lattice of roasted red peppers filled in with a five aged-cheeses blend. Simple, yet popular.

My favorite is the taco pizza. It's spiced ground beef and tomatoes, onions and jalapeños with cheddar and Colby cheeses on top of even more cheese, and it's a sight better than any other taco pizza I've ever had.

The Mileses do believe in the concept of families enjoying pizza together, and they make a special "family sheet" pizza. It's a seventeen- by twenty-five-inch pizza that comes in twenty-four square slices, and it fills the box.

THE BACK FORTY

A little further down the road is Mountain Home, which boasts a second Nima's Pizza, as well as a little country café named Brenda's. But there's one place that's been going strong for more than thirty years now that's gained an impressive reputation.

Don Houser bought the old Kettle Restaurant in Mountain Home in 1980 with a couple of partners. The next year, his wife, Opal, retired from teaching, and together with Don and their daughter Karla, they bought out the other partners.

When Don passed away, their other daughter Lisa stepped in and kept the original idea going, a community restaurant where you can get a hot meal and a cold beer that's consistently good. The signature dish is the two-fisted, half-pound burger known as the Barnbuster. Cooked on a massive griddle in full view of the restaurant's bar, this nicely spiced burger is served on a sesame seed bun, a one-two punch of beef and bread that's the go-to for diners who know the place well.

It's also known for a selection of "Ozark Mountain Meals," including the Forty Woody Platter, which is one of those grilled patties under a pile of lettuce, cheese, tomatoes, onions and crumbled tortilla chips served with or without chili.

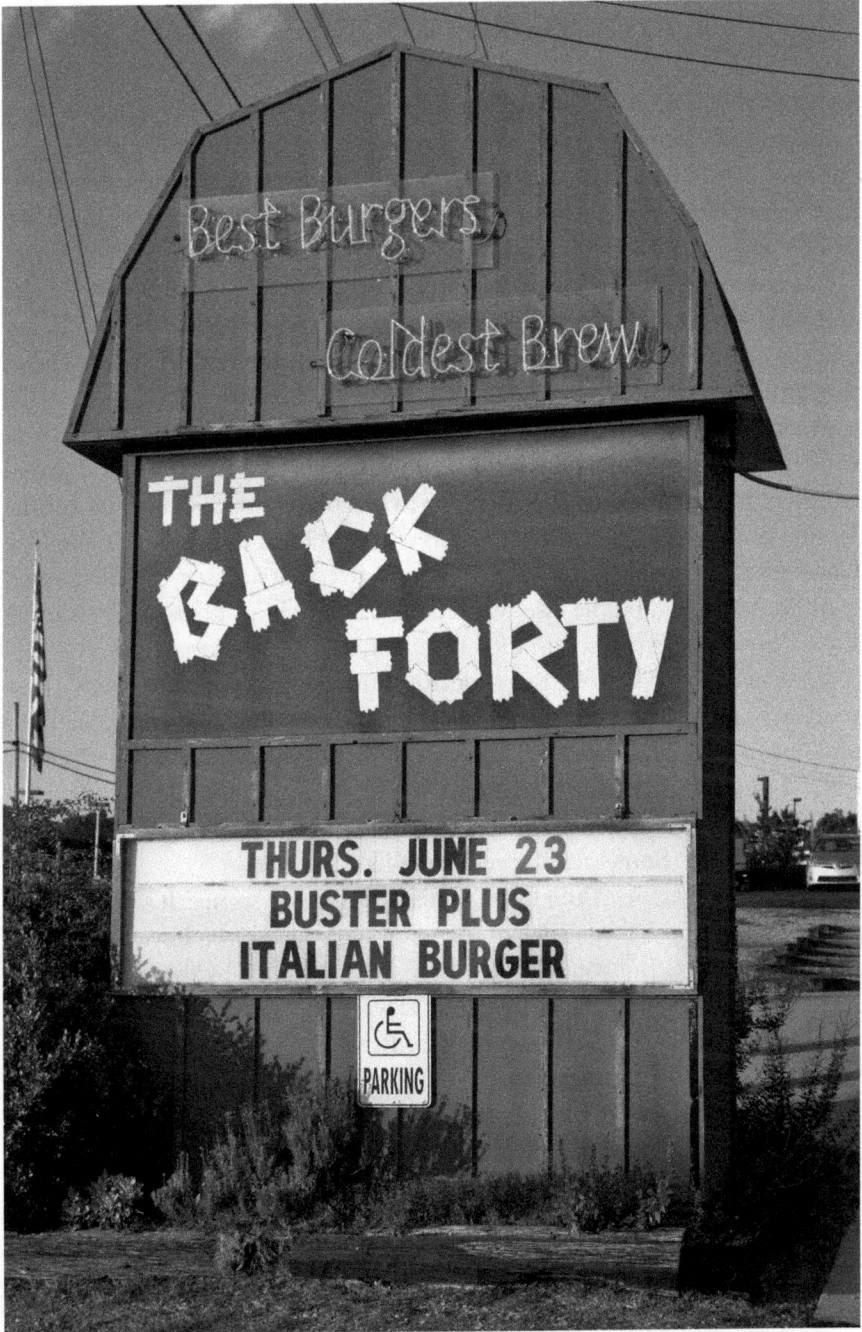

The Back Forty in Mountain Home. *Grav Weldon.*

CAROL'S LAKEVIEW RESTAURANT

Snowbirds—we get a lot of them here in Arkansas. And north-central Arkansas is packed with them, not just the expected folks from the Midwest and Chicago, but also ones from Florida and Georgia and along the Gulf Coast. My home state's moderate temperatures and four very different seasons are very attractive to folks and, especially in this little pocket in north-central Arkansas, to golfers.

Cherokee Village is home to a couple of great courses—the South Course and the North Course—and there are a couple more courses less than ten miles away in Horseshoe Bend. The planned community with its three lakes is quaint and beautifully comfortable.

When I worked at Today's THV, I made the acquaintance of a gentleman by the name of Cyril Bertram. He and his wife, Linda, decided to move from their home in Wisconsin to this place after looking all over the United States for a good place to retire. Cy had been a member of the U.S. Coast Guard Auxiliary, and after his forty-five years of service, he wanted comfortable living, but he also wanted life on the water. That he got, trading Lake Winnebago in Wisconsin for Lake Sequoyah in Arkansas.

I learned about Carol's Lakeside Restaurant from Cy, about how these retirees would get together and have breakfast or lunch on a regular basis and how they'd amalgamated. You can walk into the restaurant overlooking Lake Thunderbird today and find clusters of retirees gathered at tables, sharing stories underneath more Coca-Cola décor than you may ever have seen in your life. Sometimes, it gets quite loud.

Cy passed away in 2008, but Carol's is still going strong. It's not the sort of place you'll find if you stick to the main highways—you have to know it's there to get there. But you'll know you're there instantly by the strange shape of its roof—two curved sides like a sumo wrestler's hairpiece, painted gold.

The food hasn't ever really changed. Breakfast omelets are packed with cheese, burgers are ample at lunch and there are always fantastic pies in the pie case. Carol's does offer a lot of healthier options as well and has become known for its sugar-free pies.

MEACHAM'S FAMILY RESTAURANT

Of course, one restaurant does not a community make. On the main drag, you'll find everything from pizza joints and Chinese buffets to Mexican

Carol's Lakeview Restaurant in Cherokee Village. *Grav Weldon*.

Breakfast at Meacham's Family Restaurant in Ash Flat. *Kat Robinson*.

standards, and if you journey down to Ash Flat and turn off on U.S. 412, you're a quarter mile from the largest biscuits in the state of Arkansas.

The place is Meacham's Family Restaurant. Back in the 1970s, it was called BJ's Drive-In, but now it's named after the family who runs it. Inside, the entire interior of the dining room is wood clad, from walls to ceiling, and the crossbeams are "branded" in various ways.

And there are birdhouses. Somewhere, along the way, I suspect a family member was a collector.

Lunch and dinner are great enough, and all the potato products are made from scratch when you order.

But all you really need is a biscuit and gravy because those biscuits are big as a baby's head, better than four inches square and about two inches high. To be honest, I'm surprised that the folks there haven't started offering a sandwich on them. They're soft, wheaty and fluffy, and they really do a breakfast make.

Chapter 11

THE OLDEST SODA FOUNTAINS IN ARKANSAS

The oldest place to consume sustenance in the state of Arkansas is not a restaurant. It's not a bar, bakery or candy shop, either. It's a soda fountain.

If you think about it, that makes a bit of sense. Soda fountains are often found in pharmacies, and considering how pharmacists compounded prescriptions, the idea of putting together a series of cold or wet ingredients for pleasurable consumption wasn't that far off. The period we're talking about was a time when for many people, a trip into town was perhaps a weekly or bi-weekly affair. The trip might be combined with a visit to a dry goods store, and before heading back to the farm, if things had been going well, it might be a good opportunity for a treat for the family. What better than the exotic treat known as ice cream?

FUTRELL'S PHARMACY

The oldest of all the soda fountains still operating in Arkansas today is Futrell's Pharmacy in Pocahontas. This is about as far as you can get to the edge of the Ozarks. In fact, just down the hill from the place, a block down from the town square where it sits, lies the Black River and, across it, the edge of the Mississippi River Alluvial Plain—or, as we know it, the Delta.

Futrell's still operates as a full pharmacy, but in the front, you'll find the small red and white soda fountain. Here's where more than a century of

Futrell's Pharmacy in Pocahontas. *Grav Weldon*.

diners have come to have a phosphate or a milkshake, catch up on gossip and relax before heading home.

The Black family first opened the pharmacy and soda fountain in either 1872 or 1873. It moved to its current location in 1895. The original building here was two stories, but after a fire, it was rebuilt as a single-story unit.

THE OZARK CAFÉ

Futrell's is not the only soda fountain by far. Over in Jasper, the Ozark Café has been in operation since 1909. It's changed hands several times. It did close down for a while during the Second World War, which is all that keeps it from being the second-oldest continuously operating restaurant in the state (after the White House Café in Camden), but for the most part, it's always been there.

Inside the Ozark Café in Jasper. *Grav Weldon.*

Walk in today, and it appears to have been decorated over the generations, with an ancient backbar and other paraphernalia. But that's not really the case. Twenty years ago, the place was a tiny hole in the wall with a suspended ceiling and pretty plain interior. The reclaimed nostalgia of an entire town has been produced here by Tim and Mona Ray, who moved to Jasper in 1999 to give their kids a chance to "grow up normal." They started by building space on the same block, creating a sandwich shop, knocking a hole in the wall after purchasing the Ozark Café and revitalizing it, creating a stage area, a pizza shop and even a bed-and-breakfast. Today, it's a destination that—yes, Virginia—includes a soda fountain featuring all those great ice cream delights of a generation past.

How do you give a restaurant like that a bit more gravitas, a bit more weight and age to its atmosphere? You ask the community for memorabilia. And it is there, through photos on every wall, under the glass tops of tables—everywhere. You find ways to utilize reproduction booths and backbar. And you employ whole generations of families.

And then you get folks to come in, and there are always folks at the Ozark Café. They come for the eclectic menu, which includes everything from catfish and hushpuppies to a deep fried burger and the Excaliburger, a hamburger with a bun that consists of two grilled cheese sandwiches. You serve fried pickles and chocolate gravy and you make it well known that your location is friendly for folks with families or riders of motorcycles. And you welcome the folks who live around you. The Ozark Café didn't survive this long without doing things right.

FAMILY SHOES AND DRY GOODS

In Calico Rock, just north of the White River on the main stretch, you'll find Family Shoes and Dry Goods. Yes, it's a shoe store—dating back to 1947—but it's also home to a soda fountain where you can rub elbows with the locals and hear tales about the ghost town that's completely surrounded by the city. That's no joke—about six blocks of Calico Rock have been abandoned, and you can take a look through at your leisure. There's everything from an old auto dealership to an old feed-and-seed, a funeral home, an icehouse and even the original town jail. It's all behind Peppersauce Alley, and the Family Shoe folks can send you in the right direction.

Newton's Pharmacy

While at Arkansas Tech in Russellville, I became acquainted with Newton's Pharmacy. The old stalwart on Main Street was opened in 1970 by Billy Newton. It's still primarily a pharmacy, but the more modern backbar and counter are the perfect spot to get a chocolate soda or a Coke float in the middle of summer.

Palace Drug

Mammoth Spring has its own soda fountain within spitting distance of the Missouri border. The current Palace Drug was opened in the 1980s down the street from Fred's Fish House (you might have seen it in Anthony Bourdain's *No Reservations*), but the original pharmacy and soda fountain of that name in Mammoth Spring dates back to 1885. Inside its wood-paneled interior, you can have a seat and lunch on sandwiches and an incredibly good strawberry-pecan salad. Add in the marvelous malts—yes, they give you the old metal malt shop cup along with your confection—and you have perfection, even if the bar is partially made of that strange black Naugahyde so reminiscent of the 1970s.

Woods Old-Fashioned Soda Fountain

One of the state's most distinctive soda fountains sits a block off the town square in Mountain View. Any weekend night—or summer evening—the place is packed with families seeking a sweet treat to enjoy while taking in the pickin' on the park nearby.

Woods Old-Fashioned Soda Fountain is at least sixty years old, but the exact date the original drugstore and pharmacy opened hasn't been penned down. Dana Woods knows he bought the store from Joe Wyatt in January 1986, that Joe had the store for more than thirty years before that and that Joe bought the store off someone else.

The building, though, is newer. Dana and Annette had the new place built in 1993, incorporating a century-old soda fountain bar and backbar, designed to look like it had been standing there for a hundred years or more.

Inside Woods Old-Fashioned Soda Fountain in Mountain View. *Grav Weldon.*

Inside the two-story brick edifice are all the things you'd expect with a soda fountain: the old wood-and-mirror backbar, stools, tile floors and nostalgic memorabilia on every wall and every shelf.

Just a short while back, the pharmacy part of the operation was closed, so now it's just a soda fountain. This one's unusual in the fact that every ice cream is handmade right there. And what spectacular flavors: from chocolate chip cookie dough, peach and strawberry to Almond Joy, Nutella, pistachio nut and Hunter's chocolate—each rich and delightful. Sixteen flavors are available at any particular time.

Any sort of ice cream you can imagine can be made right here. Sodas, shakes, old fashioned and phosphates are all on the menu. And then there's a house specialty you just can't find anywhere else, with an amazing name to boot.

> *When we were building the new building, we were sourcing ingredients for recipes. We were looking for nostrum bitters. One night, my wife, Annette, had a dream. She was at an old soda fountain visiting with the old soda jerk. He added something to a drink. She asked what it was, and he told her nostrum bitters. When Annette asked where he got them from he said*

the liquor store. Annette also asked, "What are you making?" He said, "A raccoon bear claw wa wa." When Annette asked what all was in it, he told her.

Annette woke up and wrote all this down. When we recently started making our own artisan ice cream, Annette formulated an ice cream for this treat she learned about in the dream. So we now make Raccoon Bearclaw Wa Wa.

Of course, I had to do extensive research for this book. So Grav and I made our way to Mountain View to give this thing a shot.

The first thing you should know about the Raccoon Bearclaw Wa Wa is that it's about a foot tall. There's so much there that it overfills the glass and runs out on the plate below. It starts with a chocolate shell ice cream, marshmallow fluff and homemade salted-caramel sauce. Then whipped cream, more ice cream, hot fudge and the kitchen sink are added. The overall experience is like eating cake batter from a bowl, and between the two of us, we could not even finish it. As it was, it took a good bit of walking around before the sugar buzz wore off.

Next time we go, I'm thinking an Almond Joy milkshake or something slightly smaller.

Chapter 12

THE OZARK HOLLOWS AND HIGHWAY 5

Highway 5 has changed courses so many times over the years that someone who visited seventy-five years ago might have a different line on his or her mental map than someone who came fifty years ago, or even twenty-five. Though there's a section that runs from the north side of Hot Springs up through Benton and into Little Rock via Stagecoach Road (and Little Rock's Main Street Bridge secretly carries the Highway 5 assignment), the real heart of the road starts at Cabot and goes all the way to the Missouri border.

It was created in 1926, and its alignment has shifted often. In 1951, the Pulaski County section up into Faulkner County was aligned on what's now Highway 107, and then there was a break from there up to the north side of El Paso. Its route from Mountain View to Calico Rock has also been a little bit of this and that.

Today, Highway 5 is set, and it's known as a major lane of escape from the weary of workweek worries. On Friday afternoons and all through the temperate months, you'll see trucks pulling boats making the drive off Highway 67/167 at Cabot up to Greers Ferry Lake and music lovers rolling in from both north and south making their way to Mountain View for the Ozark Folk Center and all the festivals around downtown. And you'll find some of the state's most comfortable restaurants.

RED APPLE INN

Many places in Arkansas have connections with America's forty-second president, Bill Clinton. But there's one place in Arkansas that's an important place for the thirty-fifth, John F. Kennedy. Let me explain.

Construction began on Greers Ferry Dam in 1959 under the auspices of resident engineer Carl Garner (a fascinating gentleman who will engage you in marvelous stories even today at the mature age of ninety-eight). Completed in 1963, Greers Ferry today is actually two lakes plus the straight called the Narrows that together cover about forty thousand acres.

John F. Kennedy came to Cleburne County to dedicate the dam on October 3, 1963—his last public appearance before his fateful trip to Dallas. There are great efforts underway today to create a water garden in his honor to commemorate the fiftieth anniversary of the dam's construction and dedication.

Herbert Thomas, the man who incorporated First Pyramid Life and helped to form the First Arkansas Development Finance Corporation, took a chance on the lake before it was formed. See, the Flood Control Act in 1938 had already paved the way for a dam on the Little Red River, but it took decades to figure out where that dam was going to go and how much land it was going to hold back. Prospectors bought up a good portion of the land around the area in the 1940s, but by the mid-'50s, they sold out, not knowing when or if anything was going to happen. Thomas came in and bought five hundred acres of ridge top, and to make sure he didn't lose access to any of it should a portion become submerged and the rest become an island (islands within Army Corps of Engineers lakes can't be owned by anyone), he made sure to get a causeway built through the land. When the lake filled, he had a stretch that tied the main portion of his property to what he owned on Eden Island.

Thomas sold some of that land for vacation homes. He also built a lodge and restaurant that opened in 1963 and burned the following year. No matter, the next lodge and restaurant opened in 1965 and are still operating to this day as the Red Apple Inn.

It's had its share of owners and success stories. (You'll recall the story of the Smiths and Lambrecht Gourmet in the candy chapter.) In 1995, Dick and Patti Upton purchased the Red Apple Inn.

By that point in time, the Red Apple Inn had lost some of its initial luster. The Uptons poured heart and soul into the resort, spending more than $4 million to update its lodge, golf course, conference center and restaurant.

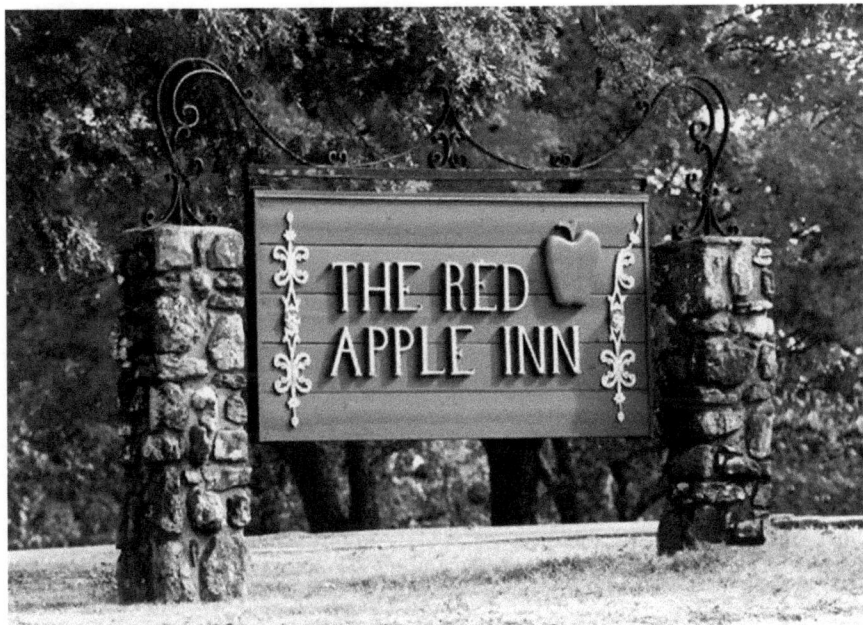

The Red Apple Inn in Heber Springs. *Courtesy the Red Apple Inn.*

And it shows. Today, the Red Apple Inn is considered one of the top resort getaways in the state.

You don't wear cutoffs and tennis shoes to the restaurant. There's a dress code, and thank heavens for that. Dinners and breakfasts alike are served off fine crystal and china, and the views over the lake are stunning. It's common to capture glimpses of bridal parties on the weekends, and in the evenings, you'll see couples celebrating the best occasions of life at tables for two.

Of course, the food today is certainly something to celebrate: prime rib, wood-grilled salmon with Jack Daniel's glaze, grilled salmon with caramelized-jalapeño bacon and balsamic glaze, Arkansas "Hog Wings" (barbecue-glazed miniature pork shanks) and fried green tomatoes with lump crab rémoulade.

And then there's the famed sticky pudding cake with fresh caramel sauce, which the Red Apple Inn has graciously shared for this book.

STICKY PUDDING CAKE WITH FRESH CARAMEL SAUCE
RED APPLE INN, HEBER SPRINGS

Sauce:
8 ounces butter
14 ounces brown sugar
8 ounces cream

Cake:
6 ounces dates
1 teaspoon soda
10 ounces boiling water
2 ounces butter, melted
3½ ounces brown sugar
1 teaspoon vanilla
1 each egg
7 ounces flour
1½ teaspoons baking powder

Bring butter, sugar and cream to a boil over medium-high heat for five minutes, until mixture begins to brown and thicken. Remove from heat and pour some of the sauce into small ramekins, small Bundt cake pans or a large, round casserole that has been buttered; reserve the rest.

Preheat oven to 350 degrees.

Pit dates and toss in baking soda. Pour hot water over dates and allow to cool.

Combine butter, brown sugar and vanilla and beat until the mixture is creamed. Add egg and stir in the date mixture. Sift flour and baking powder together and fold into mixture until everything is incorporated. Pour into pans.

Bake 10 minutes at 350, and then turn oven down to 315 degrees for 10 to 15 minutes for ramekins or small pans (50 minutes for large pans), until toothpick inserted into middle comes out clean. Remove from oven, invert onto serving dish and cover with remaining sauce. Serve hot.

THE POT O' GOLD AT LINDSEY'S RAINBOW RESORT

On the other side of Greers Ferry Dam lies the Little Red River, a brisk stream that's known for its brown trout. Indeed, until the fall of 2009, the largest brown trout ever caught was by Rip Collins in 1992—a forty-pound, four-ounce monster he happened to bring in on an ultralight rod.

Several fish camps lie along this section of the stream, including one owned by the Lindsey family. Lindsey's Rainbow Resort was founded in 1965 by Bill and Mavis Lindsey, affectionately known as Pop and Nana. Their "dream on a dirt road" started off as a dock with five slips and a couple cabins for trout fishermen before trout was even stocked in the river.

The story goes that the Arkansas Game and Fish Commission had tried to get moss to grow for the trout once the dam went in, but it wouldn't stick. Bill Lindsey wasn't just going to wait for something to happen. He and AGFC trout biologist Jim Collins went north to the Spring River, collected moss,

Then governor Bill Clinton and Bill Lindsey of Lindsey's Rainbow Resort. *Courtesy Lindsey family*.

brought it back and sprigged it out on the Little Red, the same way you get grass to grow and cover a lawn. It worked, and two years later, trout were successfully introduced.

The resort grew from its modest beginnings. Cabins were built over the decades, along with a swimming pool, a conference center, a restaurant and the marina itself. Bill and Nana's kids, Billy and Terri, took over, and the resort continued on. Lots of people came through, including local celebrities such as radio guy Sonny Martin, meteorologist Tom Brannon, magician Derrick Rose, game and fish guy Steve "Wildman" Wilson and this guy named Bill.

But at forty-five years in, Lindsey's almost became a part of the past. With the passing of both Billy's father and his wife's father, too, the family considered whether it was time to move on. The resort went up for auction in June 2010, but with no acceptable bids, the Lindseys decided to rededicate their efforts. They've since put in a new store, renovated and expanded The Pot o' Gold Restaurant and tackled running the place with a brand-new point of view.

And it's working. The trout are biting, the guests are coming and business is doing better than it has in quite some time.

The restaurant is usually busy, serving up good breakfast (with chocolate gravy and biscuits among the offerings) and dinner. Lindsey Cole, Sonny and Terri's son, runs the restaurant, and three nights—and three following breakfasts—each week, there's family and friends and new friends from the guests and the folks who fish the Little Red River. Get your trout cooked up there, try a rib-eye or some catfish and save room for fried pie à la mode.

Brother's B-B-Q

Sometimes, fate puts you where you need to be. For Larry Cordell, that place was Heber Springs. And for Heber Springs, that's a blessing paid out in barbecue and good will.

Larry runs a place called Brother's B-B-Q. But he started out in aviation. After runs with an airline in Dallas and a similar aviation situation in Memphis, he ended up managing a tool store in Heber Springs. That didn't work out so well.

He chose Heber because the place had a hold on his heart. His family used to come to Heber Springs for vacations, for the beauty of the place and

Brother's B-B-Q in Heber Springs. *Kat Robinson.*

the excellent fishing. He jumped into that new career for the opportunity to spend more time there.

As I said, the tool franchise didn't work out for Cordell, so he ended up taking another job at the Eden Isle marina. That job worked out all right for a while, and on the weekends, he'd grill out with his fellow co-workers. Thing is, Larry Cordell had a gift for creating some gastronomic grilling goodness, and within a short time, the folks who ran the Eden Isle resort started throwing money his way to help him supplement the pork butts and ribs he threw on the barbecue with shrimp, frog legs and crab.

Cordell will tell you a couple different things in conversation, if you get the chance to sit down with him in his restaurant today. One of those things would be how breathtaking the Heber Springs area happens to be, and I agree with him on that. The other would be just how hard it is to start a business in the community. Sure, for five months each year from spring to early fall, the town booms with folks coming in to fish and relax along Greers Ferry Lake and the Little Red River. But those other seven months can be harsh, with just the locals available to drop in. He related to me during my visit how hard it was and mentioned a running stream of individuals who had sold everything to come run a store or a shop in town, only to lose their shirts when winter came.

Strangely enough, that's how Larry Cordell ended up back in Heber Springs. Word of his grilling and smoking expertise got around, and a couple of brothers who barbecued heard that word. They owned Brother's B-B-Q and did not have the success they had hoped for. They contacted Cordell and asked him if he'd like to buy their place. He refused, but they wouldn't take no for an answer. They showed up on his doorsteps with the keys and told him Brother's B-B-Q was his.

They were generous; they left him with enough money to get started, to keep the power on and to make his first food order. So in 1989, with no previous restaurant experience and a lot of goodwill from family and friends, Cordell took on the job and got started.

He did just fine. He was smart, too, playing to his constituency, which happened to be heavy on people who fished. He printed his menu on the back side of a map of the lake, and he'd share with his customers the best places on the lake to go, when to go and what to expect when they got out there. Add in the fact that he did a superb smoke on his meat and never made up that 'cue before it was ordered, and a fine reputation was born.

For fourteen years, Cordell's place did great business. But a fire took it down to the ground. That didn't stop him. He got a trailer and continued selling barbecue for a couple years before finding the place the restaurant's set up in now, along the bypass. Inside today, the place looks like a lot of other good old-fashioned barbecue joints: rustic, tin, photos on the wall and sauce on the table.

It's a good 'cue, too. The pulled pork has notoriety around these parts, hickory smoked and delicious. The ribs are legendary, and the other offerings are just as good. Some swear by the slaw. I found I really liked the mayo version, but the tart and vinegary version is also fantastic. Lots of sides are offered, including potato salad, baked beans, fries and corn on the cob. The menu hasn't changed much in all that time. Cordell says the newest thing on the menu is nachos: tortilla chips piled high with shredded cheese and barbecue meat, sauce and sour cream. It's popular.

And he's popular. Cordell makes time to offer the restaurant for folks who need a place to meet and gives barbecue out for good causes. He's quiet and kind, and as I said, he knows a thing or two about fishing.

You should consider dropping in if you are in the area. The tea is cold, the 'cue is smoky and the sauce is packed with spices. Nearly twenty-five years down and heaven knows how many to go, Brother's B-B-Q is like to stay on as a Heber Springs mainstay for years to come.

AMERICAN BURGER CENTER

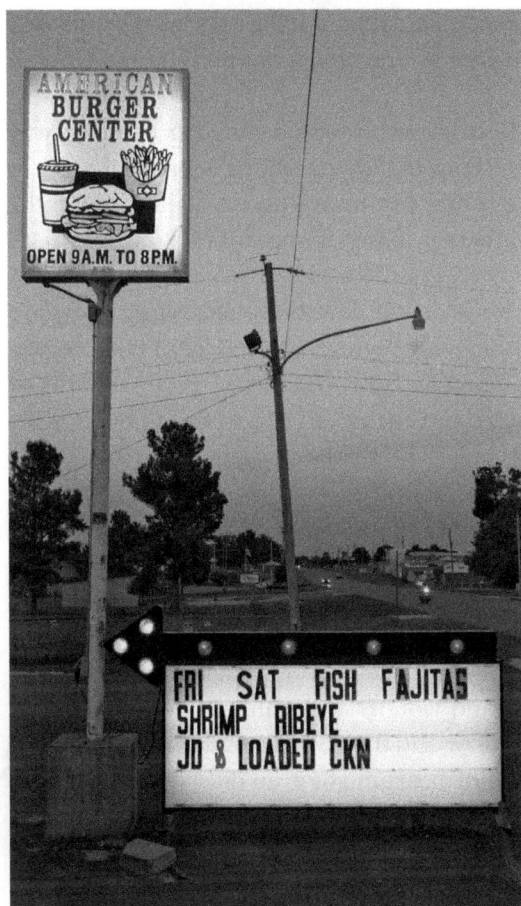

American Burger Center in Melbourne. *Grav Weldon.*

Melbourne isn't on Highway 5. You come around to it one way or another, and if you're really adventurous, you might take Highway 9 south out of town to get to Highway 5 on one of the craziest runs through the Ozarks. But to get to this comfortable little community, you really have to be trying to get there.

American Burger Center has been servicing the community for more than thirty years. But its name isn't really fitting. Yes, there are great burgers there, but the place is more about how food is interpreted in the Ozarks.

Take, for instance, the chicken-fried steak. Here it comes with a vegetable and a mound of mashed potatoes, and it's smothered in gravy. Chicken pot pie is the filling under a biscuit. There's a shepherd's pie, fried pork chops, fried catfish, Jack Daniel's–glazed chicken, fajitas, pancakes, omelets, hash browns and strawberries and cream on biscuits. Is there anything that's not on the menu here?

TOMMY'S FAMOUS A PIZZERIA

Ask about pizza in Arkansas, and invariably you'll be given directions to head to Mountain View and go west of downtown out to Tommy's Famous A Pizzeria.

Tommy's is located in an electric purplish-blue building off Highway 66, with probably the screwiest setup of any nearby restaurant. To get to the larger section of the dining room, you have to go straight through the kitchen. It's dark, it's noisy and there is always some sort of wait. But that's all fine and good.

The interior crosses and stomps on the line between college hangout, hippie haven and dorm room. Someone's written quotes from Frank Sinatra and Elvis Presley on the wall in Sharpie. Every manner of poster and photo is pasted here and there. The tables and chairs and benches and booths don't match. The paint on the walls could be considered salmon, but maybe it's different in the light that never makes it into the building. There's even a sign that proclaims, "No Attitudes No Loud Kids." The ceiling is tan, probably from years of exposure to the heat and pizza aroma from the old ovens.

You can tell the folks who have been there before. They come in loudly and are welcomed like best friends. You can also tell the ones who haven't, especially the squares, who look around like they've walked into an alley of toughs, blink to see in the dark and wonder what might have encouraged them to walk through the screen door and then off that little porch right into the squell of the oddity. The faint of heart might even duck out if they miss being welcomed by a member of the Miller family.

But if they're caught, they manage the gumption to come on in, and that's either their downfall or their salvation because once they've waited their fair share, sucked down some cola or tea or beer and had a chance to acclimate to the situation, they experience what is known as the best pizza in the Ozarks.

If they knew a little more about Tom Miller, they might not get why this place is here. If they knew a lot more, they'd get it perfectly. See, Tom Miller knew Elvis. I don't mean he met him happenstance. I mean, he actually worked security for the King in Vegas, baby, all those years ago. "The groupies scared me," he mentioned one night as we were paying up. "A lot of folks say it was Elvis and all the people around him that were scary, but what was really scary were those fans."

There's a novel to be written about how little Tommy Miller made it from being a young boy who visited the Mountain View area during his summers as a child to being Elvis Presley's security in Las Vegas. Along the way, he

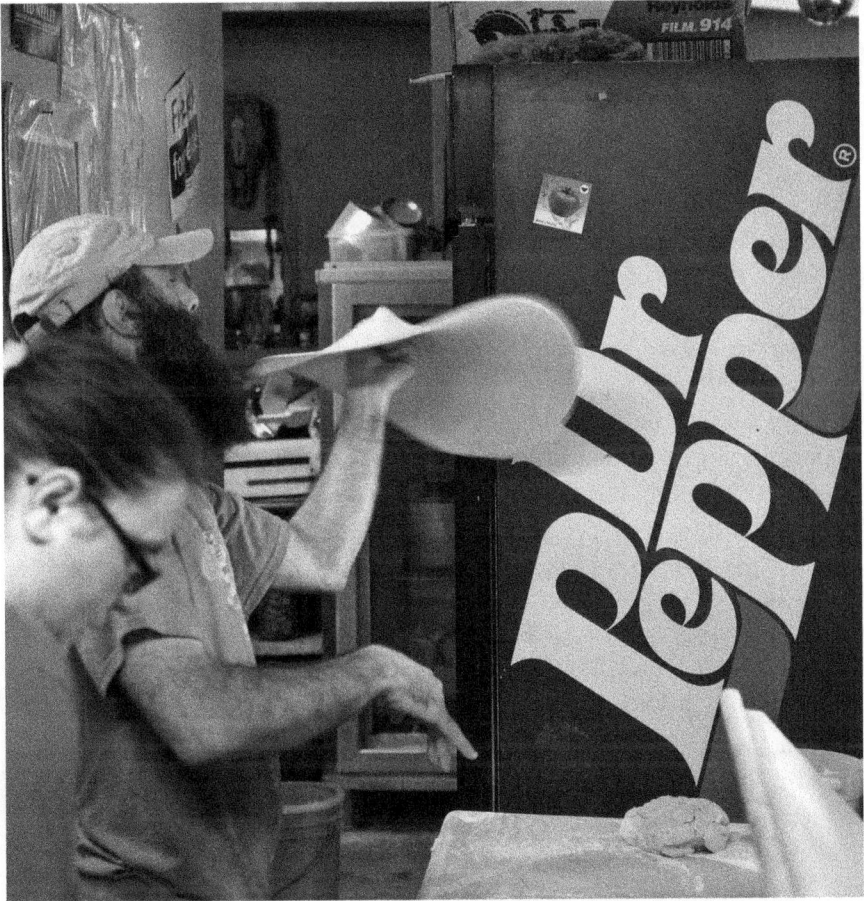

Throwing dough at Tommy's Famous A Pizzeria in Mountain Home. *Grav Weldon.*

had a sojourn in Skokie, a suburb of Chicago, and a short stay in one part of the city that even Grav describes as a "damn scary place."

I bet Tom will one day write that novel. He might even include what brought him to Arkansas to settle down and get the Vegas out of his nerves. It has to do with clean water and the clean and relaxing life you can find only in the Natural State. That was back in the late 1970s.

We pick up the story in 1991, when Tom decided to start a pizzeria. It's kinda funny. Mountain View has spent most of its existence as a quiet and quaint enclave of the Ozarks. In 1973, the Ozark Folk Center was founded. Owned by the city and operated by Arkansas State Parks, it's a haven for musicians and craftsmen who are preserving the heritage and cabin arts of the Ozarks. Its existence here and what it stirred up has developed the area into a mecca for those wanting to find their way back to a simpler place. Every Saturday night, musicians jam acoustically at Pickin' Park; various days here and there, crowds form at the county courthouse on the square to listen to music, and the audible tapping of toes on the concrete and in the grass from locals digging the groove of a century-or-more-old tune is echoed in the slap of tourists' feet on the pavement as they poke their heads into shops to check out antiques, local crafts, fudge and barbecue. At times, the heart of town seems to be hopelessly trapped in the 1940s, '50s or even earlier, with the traditions and the tunes changing little from year to year, no matter what the guests from out of town are wearing or driving.

Into this sort of atmosphere came this refuge from the quaint turn-of-the-century nature of downtown Mountain Home. Tommy's laid-back atmosphere and fantastic pizza, its location and its overall experience are all about escaping what you have to do the rest of the time you're in this world and enjoying yourself. It's an inch away from taking your shoes off and staying a while.

There's always a wait. I wasn't joking about that. When you enter, you're directed toward seating of some sort—a booth or a table or a bench. You get a menu, and you talk about what you want to eat from that menu with your friends. The large typeface almost makes up for the lack of light. Drinks are self-serve and come in paper Pepsi cups.

If you haven't figured out what you want by the time someone comes to take your order, you must have been busy talking or woolgathering because you've had the time. Then, it's another wait of fifteen to twenty minutes. You should talk with the folks who brought you—that's why you're there. Read what's on the wall, sure, but also enjoy a cold beverage and let your hair down. Tommy's is not the sort of place you visit when you're on a tight schedule.

And when you get your meal, eat it and be happy. The barbecue is all right, but if you've come to Tommy's and you don't want pizza, you are missing the big draw. Okay, you can have a hankering for a calzone instead, that's acceptable, as are the calzones themselves, which are half the size of a medium pizza pan and thick as a shoe.

The pizza, though, has that old hand-thrown Detroit-style crust, with notes of the cracker-crust you get in Little Rock at Iriana's or a number of knock-offs but thicker and pliant and resolute. The sauce is thin, a Chicago sauce hybrid that lacks the chunky marinara types so popular these days.

Cheese is stringy to a fault and the toppings are liberally applied. And that pie is hot, so don't complain when you touch the pan.

Maybe it's the wait involved that makes it just that much better or knowing that whatever you don't finish (and I'd be surprised if you were able to finish; over-ordering is almost a requirement in a place like this) will be that much better cold the next day when you're trying to rouse yourself from bed from either a late night of gabbing and listening to the pickers downtown or from having one too many of the cold brews Tommy's offers in abundance. Either way, it's a hell of a pie.

And when you get up out of your seat and head up to pay and you get the lion of a man that is Tom Miller at the cash register, be sure to ask him about Elvis. And remember that here is a man who has seen it all, been in the largest cities in the nation and had a hell of a time and chucked it all to be back here in Arkansas, where the water runs clear and—well, he'll tell you the rest.

Appendix A

RECIPE LISTINGS AND ADDITIONAL RECIPES FROM THE OZARKS AND ARKANSAS RIVER VALLEY

RECIPES THROUGHOUT THIS BOOK:

OZARK-STYLE FRIED CHICKEN AND SPAGHETTI

Chicken:

½ cup noniodized salt

2 quarts cold water

1 chicken,
    cut into 8 pieces

1 quart buttermilk

1 pound peanut or canola oil

1 cup all-purpose flour

2 tablespoons cornstarch

Salt and pepper to taste

Stir salt into cold water until dissolved to create brine. Place chicken parts in a glass bowl; add enough brine to cover completely. Cover with plastic wrap and refrigerate 8 to 12 hours. Drain brined chicken and rinse out the bowl it was brined in.

Return chicken to bowl, cover with the buttermilk, cover and refrigerate for 12 hours. Drain chicken on a wire rack, discarding the buttermilk.

In a large skillet, heat oil to medium high (will pop when flicked with water).

Sift together flour, cornstarch, salt and pepper in a shallow bowl. Dredge drained chicken pieces thoroughly in flour mixture, then shake slightly to remove all excess flour.

Put chicken pieces, skin side down, into the heated fat. Keep pieces from touching in the pan. Fry in batches, if necessary

Cook for 9 to 10 minutes on each side, until the chicken is golden brown and cooked through. Drain thoroughly on a wire rack or on crumpled paper towels before serving.

Spaghetti:

1 pound ground beef or pork (or blend of both)

2 tablespoons butter or olive oil

4 whole onions, thinly sliced

½ cup warm water

1 red bell pepper, sliced

2 cloves garlic, minced

1 (56-ounce) can chopped tomatoes, drained

2 tablespoons tomato paste

1 pound cooked spaghetti

1 tablespoon grated Parmesan cheese

In a large saucepan, heat the butter or oil over moderately high heat. Add the onions and cook until soft, about five minutes. Add water and pepper and increase heat, stirring until water evaporates. Add meat and garlic. Cook on high until meat is browned. Drain.

Return meat and vegetable mix to pan. Add tomatoes and paste. Reduce heat to moderate and let sauce simmer for 1 to 2 hours, stirring occasionally. Serve over spaghetti with Parmesan cheese on each plate beside that Ozark Fried Chicken.

FRIED PICKLES
Stephanie Wilson

1 egg
1 teaspoon dill weed, divided
6 to 8 kosher dill spears, brine reserved
½ cup cornmeal
½ cup all-purpose flour
Salt and pepper

Beat your egg, adding a ½ teaspoon of the dill weed and about a tablespoon of the pickle brine. Mix the cornmeal and flour, adding the other ½ teaspoon of dill weed and salt and pepper to taste.

Dredge the pickles in the cornmeal and flour. Coat them in the egg mixture and then dredge in the cornmeal and flour again. Freeze for about an hour. Deep fry these until golden brown and serve with ranch dressing.

FRIED PICKLES
Kat Robinson

1 cup all-purpose flour
¼ cup rice flour or
  cornstarch
1 teaspoon baking powder
¼ teaspoon salt
¼ teaspoon pepper
½ cup water
½ cup pickle juice
1 egg yolk
4 cups dill pickles, cut into
¼-inch slices
  (this works better than
  presliced hamburger dills)
Oil for frying

Sift dry ingredients together in a bowl. In a separate bowl, whisk liquids and egg yolk together and then incorporate into dry ingredients. Set in the refrigerator for 30 minutes to 1 hour.

Heat oil to 375 degrees. Working with about a ¼ of the pickles at a time, drop slices into batter and stir around. Using a slotted spoon, remove from batter and carefully place into hot oil. Fry for one to two minutes (like fried okra). Serve warm with ranch dressing.

GOULASH OR SLUMGULLION
Rebecca Lemley McGraw

3 cups water
2 teaspoon salt, divided
1 cup macaroni
1 pound ground beef

1 onion, chopped
1 can diced tomatoes
Black pepper to taste.

Heat 2 cups of water to boiling over high heat and add one teaspoon of salt and macaroni. Brown beef and chopped onion over slow fire (low heat on stove) while macaroni cooks, about 10 minutes. Drain macaroni. Add to hamburger with tomatoes, 1 cup of water, salt and pepper. Cook down.

Rebecca: As written out by my mother, Patricia Lemley, and published in the Gardner Memorial United Methodist Church cookbook (also known as "the old green cookbook") sometime in the late 1960s.

RED-EYE GRAVY
Terri Dutton

1 cured ham, sliced
1 to 2 cups hot coffee

Fry slices of ham in a skillet. (I prefer cast iron.) Be sure to use fatty ham. While you fry the ham, make a pot of coffee.

When ham is done, remove it from the skillet. Add coffee to the skillet. Stir well with the fat left in the pan. Be sure to scrap the browned ham bits off the bottom of the pan. There you go: red-eye gravy.

CHOCOLATE GRAVY

Kat Robinson

3 tablespoons butter
6 tablespoons sugar
2 tablespoons all-purpose flour

3 tablespoons cocoa
2 cups milk

Heat butter in a skillet over low heat. Mix in sugar, flour and cocoa. Slowly pour 1 cup of milk into the skillet and whisk well to remove lumps. Whisk in remaining milk, stirring constantly, until mixture is thick, being careful not to scorch. Serve hot over biscuits.

CINNAMON ROLLS OR MONKEY BREAD

Melinda LaFaver

Dough:
3 to 3½ cups flour
   (2 cups whole wheat to
   1½ cups white)
1 cup active-dry packaged
   yeast

1 pinch salt
2 tablespoons sugar
1 cup warm (100- to
   110-degree) water
2 tablespoons olive oil

Mix dry ingredients. Add water and oil and knead, adding additional water or flour as necessary until dough is smooth and elastic. Put in oiled bowl, cover and let rise in a warm place, until doubled in size.

Punch down and knead again. Then cover and let rise. (Second rising is optional.)

TO MAKE MONKEY BREAD: *Pull off small pieces of dough and roll into balls. Dip balls into melted butter and then roll in cinnamon sugar. Pile balls into buttered pan—cake pan, Bundt pan or pie pan—cover and let rise at least 15 minutes. Bake for around 25 minutes at 375 degrees. Test one to determine if more baking time is needed.*

TO MAKE CINNAMON ROLLS: *Roll dough into a rectangle, about ¼- to ½-inch thick. Cover with softened butter and sprinkle with cinnamon and brown sugar. Add nuts if desired. Roll up dough and cut into slices with sharp knife. Put in buttered pan, cover and let rise. Bake at 375 for 20 minutes or until done.*

Appendix B

AN INCOMPLETE LISTING OF EVERY CLASSIC ARKANSAS RESTAURANT IN THE OZARKS AND ARKANSAS RIVER VALLEY

178 Club
2109 Central Boulevard
Bull Shoals, AR 72619
(870) 445-4949
178club.com

1886 Crescent Hotel
75 Prospect Avenue
Eureka Springs, AR 72632
(479) 253-9766
crescent-hotel.com

American Burger Center
1215 North Main Street
  (Arkansas 69)
Melbourne, AR 72556
(870) 368-4338

AQ Chicken House
1207 North Thompson Street
Springdale, AR 72764
aqchickenhouse.net

Atkinson's Blue Diamond Café
1800 East Harding Street
Morrilton, AR 72110
(501) 354-4253
facebook.com/BlueDiamondCafe.
Morrilton

The Back Forty
1400 U.S. 62 Business
Mountain Home, AR 72653
(870) 425-7170

Barb's Coffee Shop
16 East Eighth Street
Mountain Home, AR 72653
(870) 425-5607

Barnett's Dairyette
111 West Tulsa Street
Siloam Springs, AR 72761
(479) 524-3211
facebook.com/barnettsdairyette

Bavarian Inn
325 West Van Buren
Eureka Springs, AR 72632
(479) 253-8128
eurekaspringsinn.com

Benson's Grill
2515 Rogers Avenue
Fort Smith, AR 72901
(479) 782-8181
facebook.com/bensonsgrill

Big Red Drive-In
1520 South Arkansas Avenue
Russellville, AR 72801
(479) 968-1960

Bob & Ellie's
6500 U.S. 271
Fort Smith, AR 72908
(479) 646-7559

Bob and Sandy's Beach Club
    and Bar-B-Que
5 JoJo Lane
Hardy, AR 72542
(870) 856-2593

Brenda's Country Cafe
3555 Highway 62 East
Mountain Home, AR 72653
(870) 492-5955

Brother's B-B-Q
301 Southridge Parkway
Heber Springs, AR 72543
(501) 362-5712

Brothers Cottage Café
810 Main Street
Van Buren, AR 72956
(479) 471-3335

Brown's Catfish
1804 East Main Street
Russellville, AR 72802
(479) 968-3360
browns-catfish.com

Bruce Terri Drive-In
1102 Fort Street
Barling, AR 72923
(479) 452-8121
bruceterricatering.com

Bubba's Southern Pit Barbecue
166 West Van Buren
Eureka Springs, AR 72632
(479) 253-7706
bubbasbarbecueeurekasprings.com

Café Luigi
91 South Main Street
Eureka Springs, AR 72632
(479) 253-6888

Cagle's Mill
2407 North Arkansas Avenue
Russellville, AR 72802
(479) 968-4300

Calico County
2401 South 56th Street
Fort Smith, AR 72903
(479) 452-3299
www.calicocounty.net

Carol's Lakeview Café
200 Iroquois Drive
Cherokee Village, AR 72529
(870) 257-3595

Catfish Cove
1615 Phoenix Avenue
Fort Smith, AR 72901
(479) 646-8835

Catfish Hole
24 Collum Lane West
Alma, AR 72921
(479) 632-9718
thecatfishhole.com

Catfish 'N
210 Dardanelle Dam Road
Dardanelle, AR 72834
(479) 229-3321
catfishn.com

Chuck Wagon Restaurant
9174 Highway 65 South
Bee Branch, AR 72013
(501) 745-8600

Cliff House Inn
HCR 31 Box 85
Jasper, AR 72641
(870) 446-2292
cliffhouseinnar.com

Coursey's Smoked Meats
152 Courseys (off U.S. 65)
St Joe, AR 72675
(870) 439-2503

Craig's Family Bakery
805 Fayetteville Road
Van Buren, AR 72956
(479) 471-8800

Crossbow Restaurant
537 North Parrott Drive
Huntsville, AR 72740
(479) 738-2422
facebook.com/CrossbowRestaurant

D&W State Line Steakhouse
21710 U.S. 67
Neelyville, MO 63954
(573) 989-3822
(on state line at Mammoth Spring)

Dairy De-Lite (Shari's)
402 West Commercial Street
Ozark, AR 72949
(479) 667-3571

Dairy De-Lite
1315 East Walnut
Paris, AR 72855
(479) 963-6011

Dairy Diner
220 East Main Street
Charleston, AR 72933
(479) 966-2254

Dairy Dip
29 U.S. 64
Mulberry, AR 72947
(479) 997-9991

Dairy Dream
1600 Highway 71 Northeast
Mountainburg, AR 72946
(479) 369-2295

Dairy Freeze
5400 Midland Boulevard
Fort Smith, AR 72904
(479) 783-2162

Dairy Freeze
1201 West Main Street
Clarksville, AR 72830
(479) 754-8009

Daisy Queen
U.S. 65
Marshall, AR 72650
(870) 448-2180

Dee's Drive-In
306 West U.S. 64
Coal Hill, AR 72832
(479) 497-1777

DeVito's Italian Restaurant
350 Devito's Loop N
Harrison, AR 72601
(870) 741-8832
devitosrestaurant.com

DeVito's of Eureka Springs
5 Center Street
Eureka Springs, AR 72632
(479) 253-6807
eureka-springs-usa.com/devito

Diamond Drive-In
1206 West Main Street
Clarksville, AR 72830
(479) 754-2160

Diamond Head
1901 Midland Boulevard
Fort Smith, AR 72904
(479) 782-2093

Dinner Bucket
19965 Arkansas 22
New Blaine, AR 72851
(479) 938-7034

Ed Walker's Drive In
1500 Towson Avenue
Fort Smith, AR 72901
(479) 783-3352

El Taco Casa
512 North Second Street
Dardanelle, AR 72834
(479) 229-2221

Emmy's German Restaurant
200 North Thirteenth Street
Fort Smith, AR 72901
(479) 242-3669
emmystoo.com

Ermilio's
26 White Street
Eureka Springs, AR 72632
(479) 253-8806
ermilios.com

Family Shoes and Dry Goods
114 Main Street
Calico Rock, AR 72519
(870) 297-8325

Feltner's Whatta-Burger
1410 North Arkansas Avenue
Russellville, AR 72801
(479) 968-1410

Ferguson's Country Store
121 Arkansas 333
St Joe, AR 72675
(870) 439-2234
buffalorivertradingco.com

Fred's Fish House
3777 Harrison Street
Batesville, AR 72501
(870) 793-2022
fredsfishhousebatesville.com

Fred's Fish House
44 Highway 101 Cutoff
Mountain Home, AR 72653
(870) 492-5958

Fred's Hickory Inn
1502 North Walton Boulevard
Bentonville, AR 72712
(479) 273-3303
fredshickoryinn.net

Futrell's Pharmacy
115 East Broadway Street
Pocahontas, AR 72455
(870) 892-5615
facebook.com/FutrellPharmacy

Garner's Drive-In
117 North Main Street
Berryville, AR 72616
(870) 423-2123

Gaston's Restaurant at
    Gaston's White River Resort
1777 River Road
Lakeview, AR 72642
(870) 431-5202
gastons.com

George's Majestic Lounge
519 West Dickson Street
Fayetteville, AR 72701
(479) 527-6618
georgesmajesticlounge.com

George's Restaurant
2120 Grand Avenue
Fort Smith, AR 72901
(479) 785-1199
georgesongrand.com

Glasgow Mexican and American Foods
411 Southeast Walton Boulevard
Bentonville, AR 72712
(479) 273-9958

Grandma's House Café
21588 South U.S. 71
Winslow, AR 72959
facebook.com/grandmashousecafe

Grand Taverne
37 North Main Street
Eureka Springs, AR 72632
(479) 253-6756
grandcentralresort.com

The Grapevine Restaurant
106 East Walnut
Paris, AR 72855
(479) 963-2413
thegrapevinerestaurant.com

Herman's Ribhouse
2901 North College Avenue
Fayetteville, AR 72703
(479) 442-9671
hermansribhouse.com

Hugo's
25½ North Block Avenue
Fayetteville, AR 72701
(479) 521-7585
hugosfayetteville.com

Jenny Lind Café
2655 Gate Nine Road
Greenwood, AR 72936
(479) 996-1099

Jerry Neel's
1823 Phoenix Avenue
Fort Smith, AR 72901
(479) 646-8085
jerryneels.com

Kelt's Pub
119 West Main Street
Altus, AR 72949
(479) 468-2413
keltspubinfo.com

KJ's Caribe Restaurant y Cantina
309 West Van Buren
Eureka Springs, AR 72631
(479) 253-8102

Kopper Kettle Candies
6300 Alma Highway
Van Buren, AR 72956
(479) 474-6077
kopperkettlecandies.com

Kopper Kettle Smokehouse
6310 Alma Highway
Van Buren, AR 72956
(479) 474-9949
facebook.com/
    KopperKettleSmokehouse

Lambrecht Gourmet
P.O. Box 262
Heber Springs, AR 72543
(501) 362-7514
lambrechtgourmet.com

Leslie Café
408 Main Street
Leslie, AR 72645
(870) 447-6101

Lewis Family Restaurant
5901 U.S. 71 Business
Fort Smith, AR 72908
(479) 646-4309

Local Flavor Café
71 South Main Street
Eureka Springs, AR 72632
(479) 253-9522
localflavorcafe.net

Loree's Cattleman's Steakhouse
304 West Main Street
Green Forest, AR 72638
(870) 438-6021
loreescattlemans.com

Madame Wu's
914 S Arkansas Avenue
Russellville, AR 72801
(479) 968-4569

Mama Z's
357 West Henri De Tonti Boulevard
Springdale, AR 72762
(479) 361-2750

Martin Greer's Candies
22151 Highway 62 East
Garfield, AR 72732
(479) 656-1440
martingreerscandies.com

Mary Maestri's
669 East Robinson Avenue
Springdale, AR 72764
(479) 756-1441
marymaestris.com

Master Chef
1225 North Main Street
Harrison, AR 72601
(870) 741-5700

Meacham's Restaurant
191 Highway 62 West
Ash Flat, AR 72513
(870) 994-2101

Miss Anna's on Towson
   (formerly Goodson's)
5001 Towson Avenue
Fort Smith, AR 72901
(479) 649-6300
facebook.com/MissAnnasOnTowson

Misty's
6542 U.S. 65
Leslie, AR 72645
(870) 447-2544

Monte Ne Inn Chicken Restaurant
13843 State Highway 94
Rogers, AR 72758
(479) 636-5511
monteneinnchicken.net

Morrilton Drive-In
1601 Oak Street
Morrilton, AR 72110
(501) 354-8343

Myrtie Mae's
207 West Van Buren
Eureka Springs, AR 72632
(479) 253-9768
myrtiemaes.com

Neal's Café
806 North Thompson Street
Springdale, AR 72764
(479) 751-9996
nealscafe.com

Newton's Pharmacy
715 West Main Street #A
Russellville, AR 72801
(479) 968-1157

Nima's Pizza
109 S School Street
Gassville, AR 72635
(870) 435-6828
nimaspizza.com

Oark General Store
10360 County Road 5440
Ozone, AR 72854
(479) 292-3351
oarkgeneralstore.com

The Oasis
53 Spring Street
Eureka Springs, AR 72632

Old Post Bar-B-Q
407 South Arkansas Avenue
Russellville, AR 72801
(479) 968-2421
oldpostbbq.com

The Old South
1330 East Main Street
Russellville, AR 72801
(479) 968-3789

Ozark Café
107 East Court Street
Jasper, AR 72641
(870) 446-2976
ozarkcafe.com

Ozark Mountain Smokehouse
1000 West Main Street
Russellville, AR 72801
(479) 968-7290
ozarkfamily.com

Palace Drug
270 Main Street
Mammoth Spring, AR 72554
(870) 625-3222

Paul's Bakery
1800 Main Street
Van Buren, AR 72956
(479) 474-7044

Penguin Ed's BBQ
6347 West Wedington Drive
Fayetteville, AR 72704
(479) 251-7429
penguineds.com

Pizza Parlour
8901 Rogers Avenue
Fort Smith, AR 72903
(479) 452-2228

Post Familie Vineyards
1700 Saint Mary's Mountain Road
Altus, AR 72821
(800) 275-8423
postfamilie.com

The Pot o' Gold Restaurant
350 Rainbow Loop
Heber Springs, AR 72543
(501) 362-3139
lindseysresort.com/pot-o-gold-
    restaurant

Red Apple Inn
305 Club Road
Heber Springs, AR 72543
(501) 362-3111
redappleinn.com

The Red Barn
3716 Newlon Road
Fort Smith, AR 72904
(479) 783-4075
Reed's Twin Burger
2400 Tulsa Street
Fort Smith, AR 72901
(479) 646-5312

Re-Pete's Place
7830 U.S. 71
Fort Smith, AR 72908
(479) 646-4333

The Ribeye Steakhouse
1400 U.S. 71 Business
Fort Smith, AR 72901
(479) 646-0933
theribeye.com

Rick's Bakery
1220 North College Avenue
Fayetteville, AR 72703
(479) 442-2166
ricksbakery.com

Rick's Iron Skillet
1131 South School Avenue
Fayetteville, AR 72701
(479) 442-2200
facebook.com/RicksIronSkillet

Rita's
10894 Arkansas 27
Hector, AR 72843
(479) 284-3000

Rock Café
355 South Main Street
Waldron, AR 72958
(479) 637-2975

Roger's Dairy Cream
102 East Walnut
Paris, AR 72855
(479) 963-2816

Rustic Inn
404 South Seventh Street
Heber Springs, AR 72543
(501) 362-2872

Serenity Farms Bakery
U.S. 65
Leslie, AR 72645
(870) 447-2211
serenityfarmbread.us

Skinny's White Spot
1701 Rogers Avenue
Fort Smith, AR 72901
(479) 783-9345

Smoke House Restaurant
701 West Main Street
Heber Springs, AR 72543
(501) 362-7733

Sparky's Roadhouse Café and
    Ultra Lounge
147 East Van Buren
Eureka Springs, AR 72632
(479) 253-6001
sparkysroadhouse.com

The Station Café
111 North Main Street
Bentonville, AR 72712
(479) 273-0553

Steffey's Pizza
627 West Main Street
Lavaca, AR 72941
(479) 674-2300
steffeyspizza.com

Stoby's
405 West Parkway Drive
Russellville, AR 72801
(479) 968-3816
stobys.com

Susan's Restaurant
1440 West Sunset Avenue
Springdale, AR 72764
(479) 751-1445

Susie Q Malt Shop
612 North 2nd Street
Rogers, AR 72756
(479) 631-6258

Taco Villa
420 East Fourth Street
Russellville, AR 72801
(479) 968-1191

Taliano's Italian Restaurant
201 North Fourteenth Street
Fort Smith, AR 72901
(479) 785-2292
www.talianos.net

Tommy's Famous A Pizzaria
West Main and Famous Place
Mountain View, AR 72560
(870) 269-3278
facebook.com/tommysfamous

Top Rock Drive In
314 U.S. 62
Alpena, AR 72611
(870) 437-5238
facebook.com/TopRockDriveIn

Two Dumb Dames
33 South Main Street
Eureka Springs, AR 72632
(479) 253-7268
twodumbdames.com

The Venesian Inn
582 West Henri De Tonti Boulevard
Springdale, AR 72762
(479) 361-2562
thevenesianinn.com

The Village Wheel
1400 Central Boulevard
Bull Shoals, AR 72619
(870) 445-4414

War Eagle Mill
11045 War Eagle Road
Rogers, AR 72756
(479) 789-5343
wareaglemill.com

Wiederkehr Weinkeller
3324 Swiss Family Drive
Altus, AR 72821
(479) 468-3551
wiederkehrwines.com

Wood's Old-Fashioned Soda Shop
301 Main Street
Mountain View, AR 72560
(870) 269-8304

The Yellow Umbrella
1608 South Greenwood Avenue
Fort Smith, AR 72901
(479) 783-7929

Yesterday's
1502 Oak Street
Morrilton, AR 72110
(501) 354-8821

Zack's Place
2913 West Commercial Street
Ozark, AR 72949
(479) 667-4701

INDEX

ABOUT THE AUTHOR
AND PHOTOGRAPHER

K at Robinson is a dedicated food and travel writer and lifelong Arkansawyer. Her credits include work with the *Arkansas Times*, *Serious Eats*, Forbes Travel Guide's Startle.com, *USA Today*'s The Point, *Deep South*, *Arkansas Life*, *Little Rock Family*, *Arkansas Wild*, *Savvy Kids*, *Food Network Magazine* and *Cat Fancy*. Her award-winning blog, TieDyeTravels.com, features tales of her journeys and experiences in Arkansas, the American South and wherever she may roam. She lives with her daughter, Hunter, in Little Rock.

G rav Weldon is a fine art photographer and digital artist currently living in Little Rock and working in the Ozarks and Mississippi River Delta documenting the food, culture and history of the American South.

Their first book, *Arkansas Pie: A Delicious Slice of the Natural State*, is available through The History Press.

For more on this subject, check out ClassicEateries.com or TieDyeTravels.com.

Visit us at
www.historypress.net

·····································

This title is also available as an e-book